The French Alphabet & Numbers

Learn French For Absolute Beginners

French Hacking

Copyright © 2022 French Hacking

All rights reserved. No part of this publication may be reproduced, distributed or transmitted in any form or by any means, including photocopying, recording, or other electronic or mechanical methods, without the prior written permission of the publisher, except in the case of brief quotations embodied in critical reviews and certain other non-commercial uses permitted by copyright law.

Trademarked names appear throughout this book. Rather than use a trademark symbol with every occurrence of a trademarked name, names are used in an editorial fashion, with no intention of infringement of the respective owner's trademark. The information in this book is distributed on an "as is" basis, without warranty. Although every precaution has been taken in the preparation of this work, neither the author nor the publisher shall have any liability to any person or entity with respect to any loss or damage caused or alleged to be caused directly or indirectly by the information contained in this book.

"One language sets you in a corridor for life. Two languages open every door along the way."

- Frank Smith

French Hacking is a revolutionary educational language learning company focused on teaching individuals how to learn French in the shortest time possible. Our mission is for our students to learn and master the French language by utilizing the hacks, tips, and tricks from the learning materials we create. We want our students to become confident in their speaking abilities as they advance their conversational skills by teaching what's necessary without having to learn the finer details that don't make much of a difference or are hardly used in the real world.

Unlike our competitors, who have books geared toward multiple languages, our language learning books are dedicated exclusively to learning French. Our focus on only one language allows us to concentrate on creating superior educational materials.

Our books are created by native French speakers and then put through a rigorous editing process with two additional native French editors and proofreaders to ensure the highest quality content. Rest assured that you are learning proper grammar and syntax as you read through our books.

There are no other books like ours on the market. Let us help accelerate your journey to learn French with our fun and effective educational materials that make learning French a breeze!

Want to receive a fun weekly email on all things French? It will include topics such as culture, festivals, facts, stories, and idioms. Scan the QR code below to join!

"One language sets you in a corridor for life. Two languages open every door along the way."

- Frank Smith

French Hacking is a revolutionary educational language learning company focused on teaching individuals how to learn French in the shortest time possible. Our mission is for our students to learn and master the French language by utilizing the hacks, tips, and tricks from the learning materials we create. We want our students to become confident in their speaking abilities as they advance their conversational skills by teaching what's necessary without having to learn the finer details that don't make much of a difference or are hardly used in the real world.

Unlike our competitors, who have books geared toward multiple languages, our language learning books are dedicated exclusively to learning French. Our focus on only one language allows us to concentrate on creating superior educational materials.

Our books are created by native French speakers and then put through a rigorous editing process with two additional native French editors and proofreaders to ensure the highest quality content. Rest assured that you are learning proper grammar and syntax as you read through our books.

There are no other books like ours on the market. Let us help accelerate your journey to learn French with our fun and effective educational materials that make learning French a breeze!

Want to receive a fun weekly email on all things French? It will include topics such as culture, festivals, facts, stories, and idioms. Scan the QR code below to join!

Table of Contents

Part 1: Alphabet	1
Introduction to French Writing	1
The French Alphabet	3
French Accents	4
Introduction to French Sounds	7
Why is Learning the IPA Important?	26
Conclusion	27
Part 2: Numbers	28
Introduction	28
Numbers in French	28
Using French Numbers in Context	39
Bonus 1: Top 101 French words	50
Bonus 2: The Adventures of Clara	79

Common Phrases

If you've bought this book at the last moment and need to learn some phrases quickly, here is a quick cheat sheet:

Bonjour, Mademoiselle (Madame/Monsieur)	Hello/Good morning, Miss (Madam, Ma'am/Sir)
Salut, ça va ?	Hi!/Hi there! How's it going? (familiar)
Ça va bien / Ça va mal	It's going well / It's going badly
Comment allez-vous ? (formal)	How are you?
Comment vas-tu ? (informal)	How are you?
Très bien, merci, et vous (et toi) ?	Fine, thanks. And you?
Pas mal, merci, et vous (et toi) ?	Not bad, thanks. And you?
Comme ci, comme ça	So-so
Bonsoir	Good evening
Bonne nuit	Good night (when departing or wishing someone a good night)
Je m'appelle Suzanne	My name is Suzanne
Comment vous appelez-vous ? (formal)	What's your name?
Comment tu t'appelles ? (informal)	What's your name?
Enchanté(e)	Pleased to meet you
Merci beaucoup	Thank you very much
De rien	You're welcome
Au revoir	Good-bye
À bientôt	See you soon

Part 1: Alphabet

Introduction to French Writing

<u>Origin of the French language</u>

French is one of the five Romance languages of the Indo-European language family (the other four are Italian, Spanish, Portuguese, and Romanian). It's derived from the Vulgar Latin of the Roman Empire, as were all Romance languages. More specifically, French evolved from Gallo-Romance, the Latin spoken in Northern Gaul. Its closest relatives are the *langues d'oïl*, or Oïl languages, a group of languages historically spoken in northern France and in southern Belgium. Native Celtic languages also had a great influence on French, particularly the ones from Northern Roman Gaul like Gallia Belgica, as well as the (Germanic) Frankish language of the post-Roman Frankish invaders.

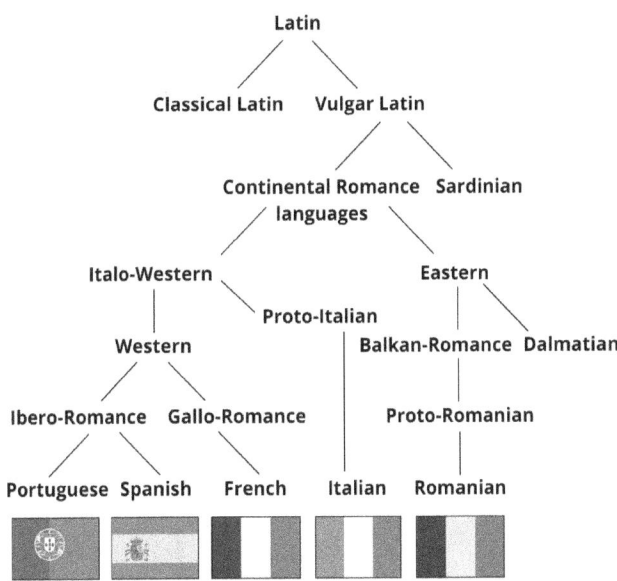

Today, given France's past overseas expansion, there are several French-based creole languages across the globe, most notably Haitian Creole. A French-speaking person or country may be referred to as Francophone in both English and French.

Below is an image showing the countries that speak French.

Origin of the French writing system

Just like English, the French writing system is based on the Latin or Roman alphabet of the Roman Empire. In addition, it uses five diacritics (the circumflex accent (ˆ), acute accent (´), grave accent (`), cedilla (ç), and dieresis (¨)) plus two ligatures (joined characters, i.e. æ, œ). The role of the accent marks is primarily creating phonetics (sounds) for words, while the ligatures "æ" and "œ" are mandatory contractions of "ae" and "oe" in some French words, as in *cœur* (heart) or *curriculum vitæ* (CV).

The first version of the French writing system (close to Latin) appears in writing in 842 AD in the Strasbourg Oaths. The text is a military pact of the alliances between two descendants of Charlemagne against their third brother to rule the inherited Empire divided among the three.

Later, the French writing system evolved with the languages of the various invaders into France, including *la langue d'oïl* (dialects of the Frankish Kingdom and Norse) and *la langue d'oc* (dialects of South and Southwestern France). "Oïl" and "oc" both mean "yes."

In regards to the Latin alphabet, its ancient origin can be traced to the Cumae form of the Greek alphabet, from which a variety of other alphabets evolved to be used in the Italic languages, a subfamily of the Indo-European languages including the Romance ones.

The French Alphabet

The word "alphabet" refers to a set of letters or symbols usually arranged in a fixed order that is used for writing the words of a particular language or group of languages. In every writing system, there are letters or characters (graphemes) for representing both consonant and vowel sounds (phonemes). Ideally, each letter represents one speech sound (grapheme-phoneme correspondence), but that's not always the case.

The current French alphabet consists of six vowels (a, e, i, o, u, y) and twenty consonants (b, c, d, f, g, h, j, k, l, m, n, p, q, r, s, t, v, w, x, z), for a total of twenty-six characters or letters. It uses accent marks as well, known also as diacritics, that create phonetic, semantic, or etymological meanings for words. Let's have a quick rundown of the letters before going through the accents that the French language has.

Letter	Pronunciation	Letter	Pronunciation
a	[a]	n	[ɛn]
b	[be]	o	[o]
c	[ce]	p	[pe]
d	[de]	q	[ky]
e	[ə]	r	[ɛʀ]
f	[ɛf]	s	[ɛs]
g	[ʒe]	t	[te]
h	[aʃ]	u	[y]
i	[i]	v	[ve]
j	[ʒi]	w	[dublǝve]
k	[ka]	x	[iks]
l	[ɛl]	y	[iɡʀɛk]
m	[ɛm]	z	[zɛd]

* [] Words you see in these brackets indicate the pronunciation of the word moving forward in the book.

Did you notice that some of the letter's pronunciation is very similar to the English alphabet?

The letters f, l, m, n, s, and z have an identical pronunciation in English while b, c, d, p, t, and v are very similar. This leaves us with a, e, g, h, i, j, k, o, q, r, u, w, x, y, the ones that may take a bit of extra effort to learn.

Fun Fact

Did you know that there are no genuine words in French containing the letter "w"?

Although the letter "w" is part of the French alphabet, all words containing this letter are borrowed from other languages like English and German. Its pronunciation closely resembles the "w" from the source language, i.e. words borrowed from English are pronounced like an English "w" (*week-end* [wikɛnd], *Wifi* [wifi], *western* [wɛstɛʀn]), while words borrowed from German are pronounced more like a "v" (*wagon* [vagɔ̃], *WC* [vese]).

French Accents

You've probably seen these funny squiggly lines when reading in French. They are called accents and they first appeared back in the sixteenth century. With the introduction of the printing press, printers looked for ways to get rid of ambiguity and redundant letters, so they created accents and other markings as a way to solve these problems. For instance, the cedilla (ç) was introduced in 1530 by the French as a way to make it clear that the "c" was soft before "a," "o," and "u" (until then, printers had used "ce," "ss," "ch," or just "c").

Now let's go through and identify these accents as they can sometimes change the sound of a word.

There are five accents total, four for vowels and one for a consonant.

Accent	Found on	Example	Pronunciation
´	é	été	[ete]
`	à, è, ù	là, père, où	[la], [pɛʀ], [u]
^	â, ê, î, ô, û	pâte, forêt, île, hôtel, sûr	[pat], [fɔʀɛ], [il], [ɔtɛl], [syʀ]
¨	ë, ï	canoë, maïs	[kanɔe], [mais]
ç	ç	français	[fʀɑ̃sɛ]

Acute accent

The acute accent (´), or *l'accent aigu*, can only be found on top of the letter "e" and is a line that goes from bottom left to top right. It changes the vowel's pronunciation to [e]. Words like *café* [kafe], *canapé* [kanape], *étudiant* [etydjɑ̃], *année* [ane], *répétez* [ʀepete], *bébé* [bebe], *été* [ete], *épaule* [epol], *créé* [kʀee], all have *accent aigu* on top of their "e."

Grave accent

The grave accent (`), or *l'accent grave*, is the little line that goes the other way, from top left to bottom right. This can be found on the vowels "a," "e," or "u," but it is most commonly used with an "e," changing the prononciation of the vowel for an open "e" sound ([ɛ]) as in the words *très* [tʀɛ], *après* [apʀɛ], *frère* [fʀɛʀ], *père* [pɛʀ], *mère* [mɛʀ], and *crème* [kʀɛm].

This accent is also used to differentiate words that have the same spelling or pronunciation but different meanings. These are called homonyms and an example is *ou* [u] which translates to "or" but with the accent above "u" (*où*) turns into "where." Another example is the word *la* [la], which translates to "the," but *là* with an accent grave on top of the "a" means "there."

Circumflex

The circumflex (^), or *l'accent circonflexe*, is a triangle without the bottom line, a bit like a hat, that can be found on top of "a," "e," "i," "o," or "u." This accent can indicate:
a) A spelling change from Latin.

b) A change in the pronunciation of the vowels "a," "e," or "o."
c) A distinction between words that would otherwise be homonyms.

In some French words, the circumflex is a linguistic reference to old French, indicating that the accented vowels used to be followed by one or more letters, often "s" or a doubled letter, which eventually disappeared. For example, the word *être* [εtʀ] used to be spelt "estre," *hôpital* [ɔpital] used to be "hospital," *âge* [aʒ] used to be spelt "aage," and *bâiller* [baje] used to be "baailler."

A little trick to understand words that you have never come across: add an "s" after the vowel with the accent and you then have the English word. For example "mât" is "mast" in English.

The circumflex also changes the pronunciation of the vowels "a," "e," and "o," but it has no effect on the pronunciation of "i" or "u" (in the past, it changed the pronunciation but it was so subtle that, at some point, French people stopped doing it). Examples of words with *l'accent circonflexe* include: *château* [ʃato], *pâte* [pat], *fête* [fεt], *dîner* [dine], *île* [il], *forêt* [fɔʀε], *hôtel* [ɔtεl], *sûr* [syʀ].

Finally, the circumflex serves also to distinguish certain pairs of identically-pronounced words, or homonyms, such as:
sur (on) and *sûr* (sure): [syʀ]
mur (wall) and *mûr* (ripe): [myʀ]

Tréma

The tréma, which used to be called "dieresis," are the two little dots (¨) you'll see above the letters "e," "i," or "u." You'll see this when there are two vowels next to each other signifying that you must pronounce each vowel separately. Some examples include *Noël* [nɔεl], *naïf* [naif], *maïs* [mais], *haïr* [aiʀ], and *canoë* [kanɔe].

Cedilla

The cedilla (ç), or *la cédille*, is a mark you will only find on the letter "c." It looks like a little 5 on the bottom of the "c." Its purpose is to make the hard "k" sound turn into a soft "c," e.g. garçon, [ɡaʀsɔ̃] *ça* [sa], *reçu* [ʀ(ə)sy], leçon [l(ə)sɔ̃], *français* [fʀɑ̃sɛ]. You'll never find it before the letters "e" or "i" since a soft "s" sound is automatically made, for example *ici* [isi] or *glace* [ɡlas].

Fun Fact

Did you know that "e" is the most common letter in French?

Trying to have a conversation in French without using it is almost impossible, as there are five different versions of this letter, the regular "e" plus other four containing accent marks, which are: é (acute accent), è (grave accent), ê (circumflex), and ë (tréma).

Despite this, a novel was written without using the letter "e." *La Disparition* is a 300-page French novel written in 1969 by Georges Perec (who, ironically, happens to have four e's in his own name). This sort of novel is called a lipogram and an example from Perec's book is: "un rond pas tout à fait clos, fini par un trait horizontal" (a circle not quite closed, finished by a horizontal line).

Introduction to French Sounds

Now, let's have a look at the alphabet from a different perspective, by classifying it into vowels and consonants.

As we mentioned at the beginning of this chapter, the current French alphabet consists of six vowels (a, e, i, o, u, y) and twenty consonants (b, c, d, f, g, h, j, k, l, m, n, p, q, r, s, t, v, w, x, z) for a total of twenty-six characters or letters. However, if we refer to the French alphabet from the phonetics point of view, that is, thinking about "sounds" instead of "letters," then we realize that there are thirty-seven sounds (phonemes), which are classified as follows:

- Sixteen vowel sounds
- Eighteen consonant sounds
- Three semi-vowels sounds

a	ɑ	ã	b	d	e	ə
ɛ	ɛ̃	f	g	ʒ	i	j
k	l	m	n	ɲ	ŋ	o
ɔ	ɔ̃	œ	œ̃	ø	p	R
s	ʃ	t	u	ɥ	y	v
w	z					

The symbols above, which are used to transcribe French sounds, correspond to the International Phonetic Alphabet (IPA). The IPA is an alphabetic system of phonetic notation created to standardize pronunciation explanations and the representation of speech sounds in written form across languages. Given that any letter may be pronounced differently in two languages, the IPA uses a unique symbol for each sound, thereby making pronunciation discussions much easier. Learning the IPA is very useful as it will give you the foundations to understand French pronunciation, particularly when you look up a new word in the dictionary to find out how it's pronounced.

Before diving into French phonetics, let's look at some basic concepts first.

What is a vowel?

A vowel is a sound that is made by allowing breath to flow out of the mouth, without closing any part of the mouth or throat.

What is a consonant?

A consonant is a basic speech sound in which the breath is at least partly obstructed. It can be combined with a vowel to form a syllable.

What is a syllable?

A syllable is a unit of pronunciation having one vowel sound, with or without surrounding consonants, forming the whole or a part of a word.

The way we form words in French is by combining letters into syllables and syllables into words.

To form syllables in French, we use thirty-seven phonemes* which are divided into sixteen vowels, three semi-vowels, eighteen consonants, and more than 130 graphemes. In comparison, English uses forty-four different phonemes and around 230 graphemes. So if you think that reading French is complicated, remember that the English language is a lot harder!

*A phoneme refers to a unit of sound in a word while a grapheme is the written code of this sound, more specifically a letter or group of letters that make a specific sound. In French, there are different graphemes for one sound. For example, the graphemes -en, -an, -em, -am, all have an identical sound, which is [ã].

Learning French phonemes and graphemes will help you with spelling and pronunciation of new words, so let's take a closer look to better understand these concepts.

French Vowels

In French, there are sixteen vowel sounds: twelve oral, and four nasal.

Oral vowels:

Vowel	Example	Pronunciation	Translation
[a]	amour	[amuʀ]	love
[ɑ] *	pâte	[pɑt] [pat] *	pastry
[e]	des	[de]	some
[ɛ]	mère	[mɛʀ]	mother
[i]	lire	[liʀ]	to read
[o]	moto	[moto]	motorbike
[ɔ]	photo	[fɔto]	picture
[ø]	peu	[pø]	little
[œ]	fleur	[flœʀ]	flower
[ə]	venir	[vəniʀ]	to come
[u]	foule	[ful]	crowd
[y]	lutte	[lyt]	fight

*Note that the oral sound [ɑ] is considered by many as a disappearing sound from the French language, and is often replaced with the sound [a] in modern French.

Nasal vowels:

Vowel	Example	Pronunciation	Translation
[ɑ̃]	plan	[plɑ̃]	plan
[ɛ̃]	fin	[fɛ̃]	end
[ɔ̃]	nom	[nɔ̃]	name
[œ̃] *	lundi	[lœ̃di] [lɛ̃di] *	Monday

What is a syllable?

A syllable is a unit of pronunciation having one vowel sound, with or without surrounding consonants, forming the whole or a part of a word.

The way we form words in French is by combining letters into syllables and syllables into words.

To form syllables in French, we use thirty-seven phonemes* which are divided into sixteen vowels, three semi-vowels, eighteen consonants, and more than 130 graphemes. In comparison, English uses forty-four different phonemes and around 230 graphemes. So if you think that reading French is complicated, remember that the English language is a lot harder!

*A phoneme refers to a unit of sound in a word while a grapheme is the written code of this sound, more specifically a letter or group of letters that make a specific sound. In French, there are different graphemes for one sound. For example, the graphemes -en, -an, -em, -am, all have an identical sound, which is [ã].

Learning French phonemes and graphemes will help you with spelling and pronunciation of new words, so let's take a closer look to better understand these concepts.

French Vowels

In French, there are sixteen vowel sounds: twelve oral, and four nasal.

Oral vowels:

Vowel	Example	Pronunciation	Translation
[a]	amour	[amuʀ]	love
[ɑ] *	pâte	[pɑt] [pat] *	pastry
[e]	des	[de]	some
[ɛ]	mère	[mɛʀ]	mother
[i]	lire	[liʀ]	to read
[o]	moto	[moto]	motorbike
[ɔ]	photo	[fɔto]	picture
[ø]	peu	[pø]	little
[œ]	fleur	[flœʀ]	flower
[ə]	venir	[vəniʀ]	to come
[u]	foule	[ful]	crowd
[y]	lutte	[lyt]	fight

*Note that the oral sound [ɑ] is considered by many as a disappearing sound from the French language, and is often replaced with the sound [a] in modern French.

Nasal vowels:

Vowel	Example	Pronunciation	Translation
[ɑ̃]	plan	[plɑ̃]	plan
[ɛ̃]	fin	[fɛ̃]	end
[ɔ̃]	nom	[nɔ̃]	name
[œ̃] *	lundi	[lœ̃di] [lɛ̃di] *	Monday

*Note that the nasal sound [œ̃] is considered by many as a disappearing sound, and is often replaced with the sound [ɛ̃] in modern French.

Every vowel sound has the following characteristics:

- It's produced by vibrating the vocal cords.
- It's pronounced with no obstruction of the throat, tongue, or lips.
- It can be a syllable on its own.

In addition to this, there are other distinctive features that play a role when articulating a vowel sound, such as sound production (oral vs. nasal), tongue position (height and backness), and roundedness. Learning about these features can help you understand how French vowel pronunciation works.

1. Sound production: oral vs nasal

According to the way a vowel sound is produced, vowels can be oral or nasal. Oral vowels are pronounced by letting the air pass through the mouth (image on the right), while nasal vowels are pronounced by letting the air pass through the mouth and nose (image on the left).

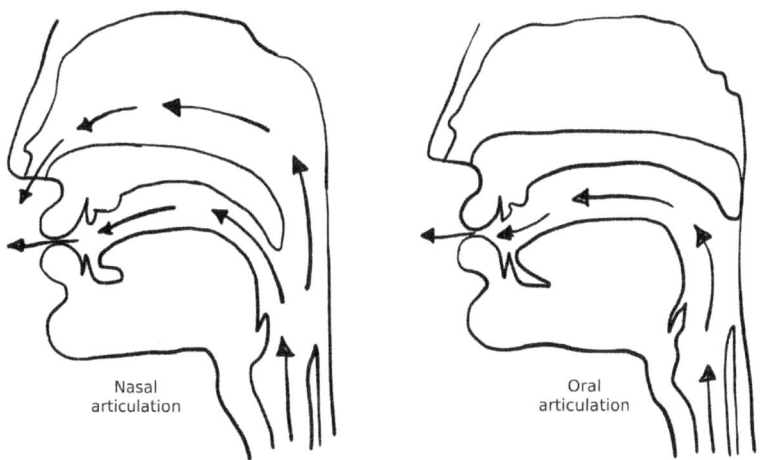

Nasal articulation   Oral articulation

Here are a few examples of oral vowels vs. nasal vowels:
   » *la* [la] (the) vs. *dans* [dã] (in)
   » *père* [pɛʀ] (father) vs. *pain* [pɛ̃] (bread)

» *sol* [sɔl] (ground) vs. *mon* [mɔ̃] (my)

2. Tongue position

<u>2.1 Height</u>: Height, or *l'overture*, refers to the vertical position of the tongue when pronouncing a vowel, relative to the roof of the mouth. Here we distinguish the "open vowels" from the "closed vowels" (*voyelles ouvertes et fermées*). Open vowels are produced with the tongue far from the roof of the mouth. They are also called "low vowels" as the tongue is found at a low position in the mouth.

Closed vowels or high vowels, on the other hand, are produced with the tongue touching or nearly touching the roof of the mouth.

In French, there are four degrees of vowel height: open, open-mid, close-mid, and close.

The following image shows the position of the tongue when articulating the most open vowel in French, which is [a] (image on the left) versus the closest vowel, which is [i] (image on the right).

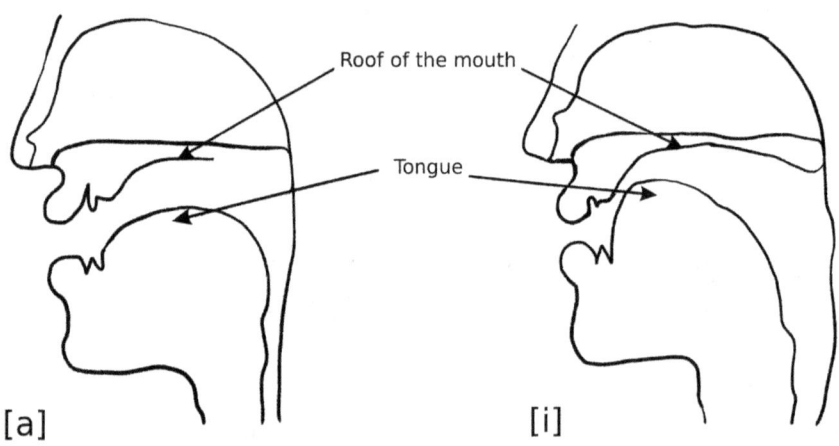

<u>2.2 Backness</u>: Backness refers to the horizontal position of the tongue when pronouncing a vowel relative to the back or depth of the mouth. Here we distinguish the "front vowels" from the "back vowels" (*voyelles antérieures ou postérieures*). In front vowels, the tongue is positioned

forward in the mouth, while in back vowels the tongue is positioned towards the back of the mouth.

In French, there are three degrees of vowel backness: front, central, and back.

The following image shows the position of the tongue when articulating the front vowel [i] (image on the left) versus the back vowel [u] (image on the right).

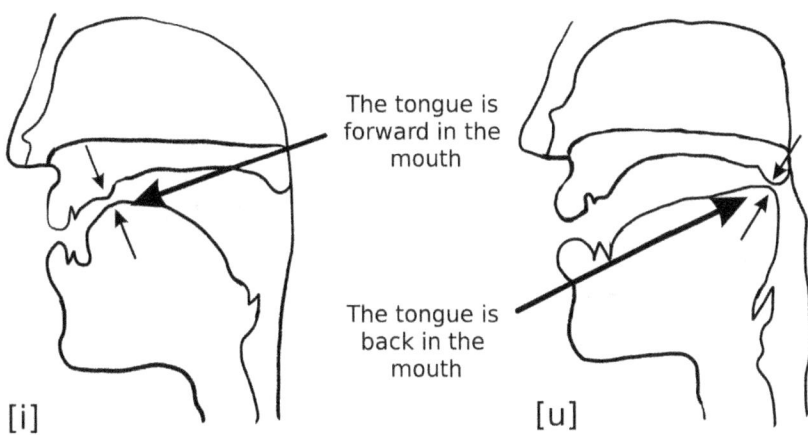

3. Roundedness

Roundedness refers to the amount of rounding in the lips when articulating a vowel. It is also known as labialization of a vowel. Here we distinguish the "rounded vowels" from the "unrounded vowels" (*voyelles arrondies ou étirées*). When a rounded vowel is pronounced, the lips form a circular opening, like when you purse your lips as if to whistle. On the contrary, unrounded vowels are pronounced with the lips relaxed.

The following image shows the shape of the lips when articulating the unrounded vowel [i] (image on the left), as in *si* [si] (if), versus the rounded semi-vowel [y] (image on the right), as in *tu* [ty] (you).

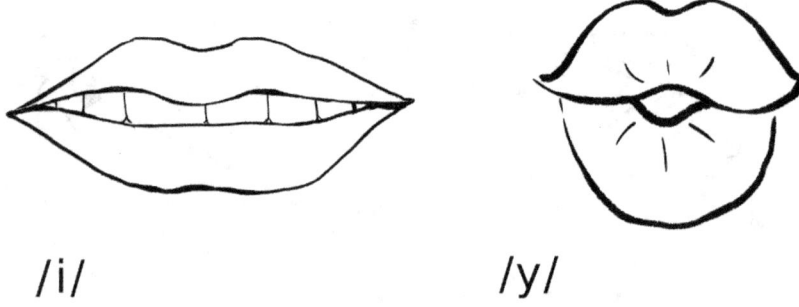

/i/ /y/

The following chart summarizes all sixteen vowels and their categorization within the distinctive features that we just discussed.

		Front		Front		Back	
		oral	nasal	oral	nasal	oral	nasal
Height	close	i		y		u	
Height	close-mid	e		ø ə		o	
Height	open-mid	ɛ	ɛ̃	œ	œ̃	ɔ	ɔ̃
Height	open	a				ɑ	ɑ̃
		Unrounded			Rounded		

Now, let's get through each of the vowel sounds individually, beginning with the twelve oral vowels followed by the four nasal ones. For every sound, we are going to name its distinctive features and the different possible spellings. Also, we will provide examples based on each possible spelling along with their phonetic pronunciation, and their equivalent in English.

Oral vowel sounds

Note: only one translation in English has been written, however, some words may have multiple meanings.

Sound	Features	Spelling	Example	Pronunciation	Translation
[a]	oral open front unrounded	a â à	<u>a</u>mour p<u>â</u>te l<u>à</u>	[amuʀ] [pat] [la]	love pastry there
[ɑ]	oral open back rounded		Note that the oral sound [ɑ] is considered by many as a disappearing sound, and is often replaced with the sound [a] in modern French.
[e]	oral close-mid front unrounded	es er ez ed ef et e é ê ai ay	d<u>es</u> donn<u>er</u> ch<u>ez</u> pi<u>ed</u> cl<u>ef</u> <u>et</u> d<u>e</u>ssiner <u>é</u>tudiant f<u>ê</u>ter l<u>ai</u>sser p<u>ay</u>er	[de] [dɔne] [ʃe] [pje] [klef] [e] [desine] [etydjɑ̃] [fete] [lese] [peje]	some to give at home foot key and to design student to celebrate to leave to pay
[ɛ]	oral open-mid front unrounded	è ê ei ai est	m<u>è</u>re <u>ê</u>tre b<u>ei</u>ge f<u>ai</u>re c'<u>est</u>	[mɛʀ] [ɛtʀ] [bɛʒ] [fɛʀ] [sɛ]	mother to be beige to do/make it is

[i]	oral close front unrounded	i î ï y	lire île maïs stylo	[liʀ] [il] [mais] [stilo]	to read island corn pen
[o]	oral close-mid back rounded	o ô au eau	moto tôt animaux couteau	[moto] [to] [animo] [kuto]	motorbike early animals knife
[ɔ]	oral open-mid back rounded	o	photo homme mort	[fɔto] [ɔm] [mɔʀ]	picture man death
[ø]	oral close-mid front unrounded	eu œu	peu œufs	[pø] [ø]	little eggs
[œ]	oral open-mid front unrounded	eu œu ue œ	fleur œuf accueil œil	[flœʀ] [œf] [akœj] [œl]	flower egg reception eye
[ə]	oral close-mid central rounded	e	ne venir acheter	[nə] [vəniʀ] [aʃəte]	not to come to buy
[u]	oral close back rounded	ou oû où	foule coûter où	[ful] [kute] [u]	crowd to cost where
[y]	oral close front rounded	u û eu	lutte flûte j'ai eu	[lyt] [flyt] [ʒe y]	fight flute I had

Nasal vowel sounds

Sound	Features	Spelling	Example	Pronunciation	Translation
[ã]	nasal open back rounded	an am en em (i)ent	pl<u>an</u> <u>am</u>bition v<u>en</u>t <u>em</u>porter cli<u>ent</u>	[plã] [ãbisjɔ̃] [vã] [ãpɔʀte] [klijã]	plan ambition wind to take away client
[ɛ̃]	nasal open-mid front unrounded	in im yn ym un um ein eim ain aim oin (i)en (y)en é(en) en	f<u>in</u> <u>im</u>pact s<u>yn</u>dicat s<u>ym</u>bole l<u>un</u>di parf<u>um</u> p<u>ein</u>ture R<u>eim</u>s p<u>ain</u> d<u>aim</u> c<u>oin</u> ch<u>ien</u> cito<u>yen</u> cor<u>éen</u> exam<u>en</u>	[fɛ̃] [ɛ̃pakt] [sɛ̃dika] [sɛ̃bɔl] [lɛ̃di] [paʀfɛ̃] [pɛ̃tyʀ] [ʀɛ̃s] [pɛ̃] [dɛ̃] [kwɛ̃] [ʃjɛ̃] [sitwajɛ̃] [kɔʀeɛ̃] [ɛgzamɛ̃]	end impact trade union symbol Monday perfume paint Reims bread deer corner dog citizen Korean exam
[ɔ̃]	nasal open-mid back rounded	on om	c<u>on</u>tent n<u>om</u>	[kɔ̃tã] [nɔ̃]	happy name
[œ̃]	nasal open-mid back rounded	Note that the nasal sound [œ̃] is considered by many as a disappearing sound, and is often replaced with the sound [ɛ̃] in modern French.			

French Consonants

Consonant sounds are articulated by blocking or hindering the passage of air through the mouth in some way. As we mentioned before, consonants can be combined with vowels to form syllables.

In French, there are eighteen consonant sounds; they all share the following characteristics:

- They are pronounced with some obstruction of the throat, tongue, or lips.
- They cannot be a syllable on their own.

Similar to vowel sounds, there are distinctive features that are part of articulating consonant sounds, such as voicing, manner of articulation, and place of articulation.

1. Voicing

Voicing (*la sonorité*) is a feature that involves the vibration of the vocal cords when articulating a consonant sound. When the vocal cords vibrate as the result of air from the lungs pushing past them, then we talk about voiced consonants (*consonnes sonores*). When there is no vibration of the vocal cords, then we talk about unvoiced or voiceless consonants (*consonnes sourdes*).

To know whether a consonant is voiced or not, you can place your fingers on your throat to feel the vibration of your vocal cords as you pronounce a consonant sound. If you feel a vibration, the consonant is a voiced one. Try this by making the sounds [b] and [p] (just the consonant sound, not the name of the letter). You should feel your vocal cords vibrate when you pronounce the [b] but not when you pronounce the [p].

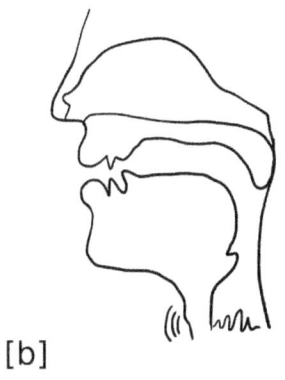
[b]
Vocal cords moving

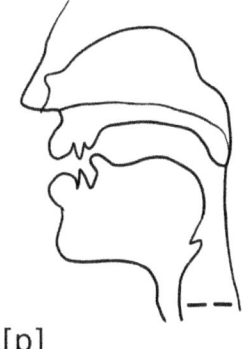
[p]
Vocal cords not moving

Below are the voiced and unvoiced consonant sounds in French:
» Voiced: [b], [d], [g], [ʒ], [v], [z], [l],[m], [n], [ɲ], [ŋ], and [ʀ].
» Unvoiced: [p], [t], [k], [ʃ], [f], and [s].

2. Manner of articulation

The manner of articulation (*le mode d'articulation*) refers to the degree of air blockage when pronouncing a consonant sound. Here we distinguish three types of consonant sounds:

2.1 Plosive: Plosive consonants, also known as occlusive or stop (*les consonnes occlusives*), are produced by blocking the passage of air. The term refers to the release burst (plosion) when articulating the consonant as a result of the tongue or lips momentarily stopping the airflow from the lungs. In French, there are six plosive consonant sounds: [p], [b], [t], [d], [k], and [g].

2.2 Fricative: Fricative or constrictive consonants (*les consonnes fricatives*) are produced by partially blocking the passage of air through an obstruction created by the tongue or the lips. In French, there are six constrictive consonant sounds: [f], [v], [ʃ], [ʒ], [s], and [z].

2.3 Nasals: When a nasal consonant is articulated, air passes through the mouth and into the nasal cavity. Nasal consonants can be considered occlusives by some because air is somewhat blocked in the mouth, but it passes freely through the nasal cavity. In French, there are four nasal consonants: [m], [n], [ɲ], and [ŋ].

2.4 Liquids: In phonetics, a liquid is a consonant sound in which the tongue produces a partial closure in the mouth. These liquid consonants can easily join other consonants to make new sounds. In French, there are two liquid consonants: [l] and [R].

3. Place of articulation

The last feature to consider when categorizing consonant sounds is the place of articulation (*le lieu d'articulation*), that is, the place where the air is blocked either by the lips, teeth, palate, velum (back of the palate), and/or the tongue. Based on this, consonant sounds can be classified as follows:

3.1 Bilabial: These are sounds that are made by touching both of your lips, top and bottom. In French, there are three bilabial consonant sounds (*les consonnes bilabiales*): [p], [b], and [m].

3.2 Labiodental: To create these sounds, the upper teeth touches the lower lip. The labiodental consonant sounds (*les consonnes labiodentales*) in French are [f] and [v].

3.3 Dental: To make dental sounds, the tip of the tongue touches the upper teeth. In French, the dental consonant sounds (*les consonnes dentales*) are: [t], [d], [n], and [l].

3.4 Alveolar: The tip of the tongue touches the alveolar ridge to make these sounds; the alveolar ridge is located slightly behind your top two middle teeth. There are two alveolar consonant sounds (*les consonnes alvéolaires*) in French: [s] and [z].

3.5 Palatal: To make these sounds, the back of the tongue is near the palate. The palatal consonant sounds (*les consonnes palatales*) in French are [ʃ], [ʒ] and [ɲ].

3.6 Velar: To make velar sounds, the back of the tongue is against the upper throat. The velar consonant sounds (*les consonnes vélaires*) in French are: [k], [g], [ŋ], and [ʀ].

The following table summarizes all French consonant sounds and their categorization within the distinctive features that we just discussed.

	Bilabial		Labio-dental		Dental		Alveolar		Palatal		Velar	
*Voicing**	V	U	V	U	V	U	V	U	V	U	V	U
Plosive	b	p			d	t					g	k
Fricative			v	f			z	s	ʒ	ʃ		
Liquid					l						ʀ	
Nasal	m				n				ɲ		ŋ	

* Voicing:
V = voiced
U = unvoiced

Now, let's get through each of the consonant sounds individually, naming their distinctive features and the different possible spellings, along with examples, phonetic pronunciation, and translation into English.

Sound	Features	Spelling	Example	Pronunciation	Translation
[p]	unvoiced plosive bilabial	p pp	<u>p</u>ays a<u>pp</u>orter	[pei] [apɔʀte]	country to bring
[b]	voiced plosive bilabial	b bb	<u>b</u>ière a<u>bb</u>aye	[bjɛʀ] [abei]	beer abbey
[t]	unvoiced plosive dental	t tt th	<u>t</u>able ne<u>tt</u>oyer <u>th</u>é	[tabl] [netwaje] [te]	table to clean tea

[d]	voiced plosive dental	d dd	danser addition	[dɑ̃se] [adisjɔ̃]	to dance addition
[k]	unvoiced plosive velar	ca co cu cc k qu	carte cours locuteur accord kilo chaque	[kaʀt] [kuʀ] [lɔkytœʀ] [akɔʀ] [kilo] [ʃak]	card lesson speaker agreement kilo each
[g]	voiced plosive velar	g ga go gue gui	gros gare goût vague guide	[gʀo] [gaʀ] [gu] [vag] [gid]	large station taste wave guide
[f]	unvoiced fricative labiodental	f ff ph	femme effet physique	[fam] [efɛ] [fizik]	woman effect physical
[v]	voiced fricative labiodental	v w	voiture wagon	[vwatyʀ] [vagɔ̃]	car wagon
[s]	unvoiced fricative alveolar	s ss sc ç ci cy ce ti+oral vowel x	sol aussi science français ciel cyclisme placer création dix	[sɔl] [osi] [sjɑ̃s] [fʀɑ̃sɛ] [sjɛl] [siklism] [plase] [kʀeasjɔ̃] [dis]	ground too, also science French sky cycling to place, put creation ten
[z]	voiced fricative alveolar	z s	zone maison	[zon] [mɛzɔ̃]	zone, area house
[ʃ]	unvoiced fricative palatal	ch sch	riche schéma	[ʀiʃ] [ʃema]	rich diagram

[ʒ]	voiced fricative palatal	j gi gy ge gea geo	jamais girafe gym manger géant géométrie	[ʒamɛ] [ʒiʀaf] [ʒim] [mɑ̃ʒe] [ʒeɑ̃] [ʒeɔmetʀi]	never giraffe gym to eat giant geometry
[ʀ]	voiced liquid velar	r rr rh	regarder terre rhétorique	[ʀəgaʀde] [tɛʀ] ʀetɔʀik]	to look soil, ground rhetoric
[l]	voiced liquid dental	l ll	lumière ellipse	[lymjɛʀ] [elips]	light ellipse
[m]	voiced nasal bilabial	m mm	famille pomme	[famij] [pɔm]	family apple
[n]	voiced nasal dental	n nn	nous donner	[nu] [dɔne]	we to give
[ɲ]	voiced nasal palatal	gn	gagner ligne	[gaɲe] [liɲ]	to win line
[ŋ]*	voiced nasal velar	ng	camping meeting	[kɑ̃piŋ] [mitiŋ]	camping meeting

*The sound [ŋ] is not a native phoneme of French, but it occurs in words borrowed from English like camping, meeting, kung-fu, and smoking.

23

French Semi-vowels

Semi-vowels, also known as semi-consonants, glides, or approximants, are sounds pronounced somewhere between vowels and consonants, as its name suggests. They're articulated by partially obstructing the passage of air through the mouth.

In French, there are three semi-vowels; each of them corresponds phonetically to a pure, normal vowel sound:

Semi-vowel	Corresponding vowel
[j]	[i]
[w]	[u]
[ɥ]	[y]

The pure, normal vowel sounds are transformed into semi-vowels when followed or preceded by another vowel, creating a diphthong.

To sum up, every semi-vowel sound has the following characteristics:

- It's pronounced with partial obstruction of the passage of air through the mouth.
- It's phonetically equivalent to a pure vowel.
- It creates a diphthong with the vowel it precedes or follows.
- It cannot be a syllable on its own.

In terms of classification, semi-vowel sounds share a common feature with consonant sounds, which is the place of articulation.

Let's have a look at each of them.

Sound	Feature	Spelling	Example	Pronunciation	Translation
[j]	palatal	i + oral vowel y + oral vowel il ill	m<u>i</u>el envo<u>y</u>er déta<u>il</u> trava<u>ill</u>er	[mjɛl] [ɑ̃vwaje] [detaj] [tʀavaje]	honey to send detail to work
[w]	velar	ou + oral vowel oi oy	<u>ou</u>est n<u>oi</u>r cit<u>oy</u>en	[wɛst] [nwaʀ] [sitwajɛ̃]	west black citizen
[ɥ]	palatal	u + oral vowel	n<u>u</u>it d<u>u</u>el	[nɥi] [dɥɛl]	night duel

<u>Pronunciation Tips</u>

- When you speak, remember to keep vowel sounds and all syllables short and clear.
- Most French vowel sounds are pronounced closer to the front of the mouth than their English counterparts.
- When articulating French vowels, the tongue and lips remain tensed.
- When articulating French consonants, the tongue always remains tensed.
- French consonant sounds, except for the "gargled" sound of [ʀ], are farther forward in the mouth than English.
- French consonants do not have an initial aspiration, but do have a slight aspiration at the end.
- At the end of words, French consonants are often silent.
- There is a slight "fall" or descending intonation on the last word of a sentence or syllable of a word.
- In yes/no questions, intonation rises slightly (example: tu arrives ?).

Why is Learning the IPA Important?

The bedrock of comprehension for any language is understanding its alphabet. Every single alphabet is different from another, whether it's in its written form or in its pronunciation. However, the IPA provides a standardized representation of sounds that makes us more aware of how words are meant to be pronounced in their native language. If you get familiar with the IPA and the phonemes related to the French language, it will give you an excellent head start in learning how to write, read, and pronounce the language.

A language's phonetic alphabet works as its building blocks. Learning how to read or write in any language without first having an overview of its sounds is like trying to build a house without setting the foundation!

Learning the basics of the IPA will allow you to recognize the symbols, as well as help you with vocabulary, grammar, spelling, and, most importantly, with pronunciation. Learning the individual sounds in French will start uncovering nuances and intricacies that are not always obvious when you're simply listening to the words, and it will help you quickly master new foreign sounds.

Fun Fact

Did you know that over 10,000 English words were actually borrowed from French?

In 1066 AD, England was occupied by French speakers. The Norman invasion had strong linguistic influences on the English language over the course of the following 300 years, shaping it profoundly. It's estimated that around 10,000 French words entered the English language after the invasion and many of them are still in use today.

Conclusion

That's it for the alphabet! Don't worry if you don't feel too confident, it takes time for this to sink in. Come back to reread and relisten to this any time. Before we finish, here are three tips and tricks that will help you on your French journey:

- Generally, you don't pronounce the final consonant in a word but there are exceptions that you will learn along the way. So if you're ever unsure, it's safer to just not say it.
- Don't assume. Just because some things are pronounced one way in English, doesn't mean they'll be the same in French. It's better to give it a go how you would expect a French person to say it, and say it in a French accent.
- Try to imitate the accent. You may think it's silly to talk with one but it's even worse if you use a heavy American, Irish, Scottish or whatever accent you have, to talk French. Putting the accent on makes you sound far more authentic.

Part 2: Numbers

Introduction

Learning numbers is an essential part of every language. When it comes to interacting with other people, numbers are undeniably important as you will use them to tell your age, to find out how much something costs, or to even exchange numbers with that cute Frenchie you've just met.

Learning how the French speak and write numbers might be a bit tedious and boring for some, but in the end it's something you need to know if you want to start communicating in French. Learning the numbers is just like learning any other kind of vocabulary, once you've memorized and practiced them, they will get easier.

In the lines that follow, we will go through numbers in French and give you some useful tricks that will help you understand how they're structured so you can memorize them more efficiently.

Numbers in French

French numbers aren't quite as straightforward as numbers in English; certain numbers simply need to be learned by heart, others follow a particular pattern, and there are a few that even require you to do a little math. Luckily, there is some logic behind their number system which, once you understand, becomes easier to remember.

First, let's differentiate between cardinal numbers and ordinal numbers. Cardinal numbers tell how many of something there are, i.e. one, two, three, four, five; they are also known as counting numbers because they show quantity. Ordinal numbers tell the position or rank of something in a list, i.e. 1st, 2nd, 3rd, 4th, 5th, etc.

We will be going over both types of numbers.

Cardinal Numbers

Cardinal numbers are used to indicate quantity, dates, times, measurements, etc. We're going to begin by learning to count to 9.999.999.999 (neuf milliards, neuf cent quatre-vingt-dix-neuf millions, neuf cent quatre-vingt-dix-neuf mille, neuf cent quatre-vingt-dix-neuf). This will give you all the numbers you'll ever need.

So let's begin!

The first thing to notice here is that, in French, a period or a space is used to separate numbers every three digits, where a comma would be used in English.

Numbers from 0 to 20

The first thing to remember with numbers ranging from 0 to 20 is that, up until 16, there is no rule. This means that you'll have to learn them by heart.

#	French	English
0	zéro	zero
1	un	one
2	deux	two
3	trois	three
4	quatre	four
5	cinq	five
6	six	six
7	sept	seven
8	huit	eight
9	neuf	nine
10	dix	ten
11	onze	eleven
12	douze	twelve

13	treize	thirteen
14	quatorze	fourteen
15	quinze	fifteen
16	seize	sixteen

And here's where it gets interesting and, in some ways, easier. For 17, 18, and 19, you just have to take the number ten (dix) and add the corresponding unit. So you end up with *dix-sept*, *dix-huit*, and *dix-neuf*. Notice that hyphens are used when these numbers are written down.

#	French	English
17	dix-sept	seventeen
18	dix-huit	eighteen
19	dix-neuf	nineteen
20	vingt	twenty

<u>Numbers from 21 to 69</u>

When you get past 20, the pattern becomes similar to what we have in English where we have a stem and add the numbers between one and nine after them using hyphens in between.

The only exception is with the "ones" where you also have to include the word "et" (and), as in *vingt-et-un* (twenty-one), *trente-et-un* (thirty-one), *quarante-et-un* (forty-one), etc. Notice that these numbers are also written with hyphens.

#	French	English
21	vingt-et-un	twenty-one
22	vingt-deux	twenty-two
23	vingt-trois	twenty-three
24	vingt-quatre	twenty-four
25	vingt-cinq	twenty-five
26	vingt-six	twenty-six
27	vingt-sept	twenty-seven
28	vingt-huit	twenty-eight
29	vingt-neuf	twenty-nine
30	trente	thirty
31	trente-et-un	thirty-one
32	trente-deux	thirty-two
33	trente-trois	thirty-three
34	trente-quatre	thirty-four
35	trente-cinq	thirty-five
36	trente-six	thirty-six
37	trente-sept	thirty-seven
38	trente-huit	thirty-eight
39	trente-neuf	thirty-nine
40	quarante	forty
41	quarante-et-un	forty-one
42	quarante-deux	forty-two
43	quarante-trois	forty-three
44	quarante-quatre	forty-four
45	quarante-cinq	forty-five
46	quarante-six	forty-six
47	quarante-sept	forty-seven
48	quarante-huit	forty-eight
49	quarante-neuf	forty-nine
50	cinquante	fifty

51	cinquante-et-un	fifty-one
52	cinquante-deux	fifty-two
53	cinquante-trois	fifty-three
54	cinquante-quatre	fifty-four
55	cinquante-cinq	fifty-five
56	cinquante-six	fifty-six
57	cinquante-sept	fifty-seven
58	cinquante-huit	fifty-eight
59	cinquante-neuf	fifty-nine
60	soixante	sixty
61	soixante-et-un	sixty-one
62	soixante-deux	sixty-two
63	soixante-trois	sixty-three
64	soixante-quatre	sixty-four
65	soixante-cinq	sixty-five
66	soixante-six	sixty-six
67	soixante-sept	sixty-seven
68	soixante-huit	sixty-eight
69	soixante-neuf	sixty-nine

Numbers from 70 to 99

Once we get to seventy, eighty, and ninety, we have to use a little math.

To say seventy, we have to say *soixante-dix*, which is like saying sixty ten in English (60+10). To say seventy-one we would say *soixante-et-onze*, seventy-two would be *soixante-douze*, and the pattern would follow all the way up to seventy-nine.

Notice that hyphens are used in all these numbers as well.

#	French	English
70	soixante-dix	seventy
71	soixante-et-onze	seventy-one
72	soixante-douze	seventy-two
73	soixante-treize	seventy-three
74	soixante-quatorze	seventy-four
75	soixante-quinze	seventy-five
76	soixante-seize	seventy-six
77	soixante-dix-sept	seventy-seven
78	soixante-dix-huit	seventy-eight
79	soixante-dix-neuf	seventy-nine

Eighty is a little tricky to get your head around at first since the French say *quatre-vingts*, which is like saying four twenties in English (4x20). A little tip to remember when writing this is that *quatre-vingts* has an "s" at the end; however, once you start counting above eighty, *quatre-vingts* loses the "s."

#	French	English
80	quatre-vingts	eighty
81	quatre-vingt-un	eighty-one
82	quatre-vingt-deux	eighty-two
83	quatre-vingt-trois	eighty-three
84	quatre-vingt-quatre	eighty-four
85	quatre-vingt-cinq	eighty-five
86	quatre-vingt-six	eighty-six
87	quatre-vingt-sept	eighty-seven
88	quatre-vingt-huit	eighty-eight
89	quatre-vingt-neuf	eighty-nine

We continue with *quatre-vingt-deux*, *quatre-vingt-trois*, etc., all the way up to eighty-nine and then for ninety we have... (Can you guess it?)

If you got *quatre-vingt-dix,* bravo! (4x20+10)

To get to ninety-nine is simple enough since you know the pattern now. You would add the number between eleven and nineteen after "quatre-vingts."

#	French	English
90	quatre-vingt-dix	ninety
91	quatre-vingt-onze	ninety-one
92	quatre-vingt-douze	ninety-two
93	quatre-vingt-treize	ninety-three
94	quatre-vingt-quatorze	ninety-four
95	quatre-vingt-quinze	ninety-five
96	quatre-vingt-seize	ninety-six
97	quatre-vingt-dix-sept	ninety-seven
98	quatre-vingt-dix-huit	ninety-eight
99	quatre-vingt-dix-neuf	ninety-nine

Cultural Fact

Did you know that other French-speaking countries like Belgium and Switzerland have a different way to count from 70 to 99?

For example seventy is "septante" in both Belgium and Switzerland. Eighty is "huitante" in Switzerland, but not in Belgium. Ninety is "nonante" in both Belgium and Switzerland.

However, if you find this too confusing, just stick to the standard French forms of *soixante-dix, quatre-vingts, quatre-vingt-dix,* and so on. You'll still be understood anyway even if you're in one of these countries!

Numbers from 100 and above

To make a larger number is very simple. You just need to learn a few more words. The ingredients you'll need to make larger numbers are:

#	French	English
100	cent	one hundred
1.000	mille	one thousand
1.000.000	un million	a million
1.000.000.000	un milliard	a billion

There are a few little rules we need to go through to sound like a native speaker when saying numbers. To begin with, there is no "un" in front of one hundred like we have in English. So one hundred and twenty is *cent-vingt*.

To make other three digit numbers all we have to do is put a number between one and nine followed by "cents." So "two hundred" will be "deux cents." We have to remember that numbers larger than two hundred will have an "s" at the end of "cents." However, when "cents" is followed by another number, it loses the "s": so "deux cents," but "deux cent un." See the following examples:

#	French	English
101	cent-un	one hundred and one
123	cent-vingt-trois	one hundred and twenty-three
200	deux-cents	two hundred
201	deux-cent-un	two hundred and one
222	deux-cent-vingt-deux	two hundred and twenty-two
357	trois-cent-cinquante-sept	three hundred and fifty-seven
799	sept-cent-quatre-vingt-dix-neuf	seven hundred and ninety-nine

| 999 | neuf-cent-quatre-vingt-dix-neuf | nine hundred and ninety-nine |

The examples above should give you the basic structure of how these numbers work.

Counting above one thousand is the same format, but you add *mille* in front of the numbers we just went through to form a four digit number. Again, there's no article or number in front of *mille* when it means one thousand. In addition, *mille* is invariable, so you don't pluralize: *deux-mille, trois-mille,* etc.

Notice that while English uses a comma separator for four digit numbers and up, French uses a period or a space, except when talking about dates where the period (or comma in English) is omitted.

Check the following examples:

#	French	English
1.000	mille	one thousand
1.001	mille-un	one thousand and one
1.945	mille-neuf-cent-quarante-cinq	one thousand nine hundred and forty-five
2.000	deux-mille	two thousand
2.200	deux-mille-deux-cents	two thousand two hundred
2.203	deux-mille-deux-cent-trois	two thousand two hundred and three
3.479	trois-mille-quatre-cents soixante-dix-neuf	three thousand four hundred and seventy-nine
10.069	dix-mille-soixante-neuf	ten thousand and sixty-nine
100.000	cent-mille	one hundred thousand
999.999	neuf-cent-quatre-vingt-dix-neuf-mille-neuf-cent-quatre-vingt-dix-neuf	nine hundred and ninety-nine thousand nine hundred and ninety-nine

One thing to keep in mind is that all these numbers are hyphenated, except when talking about euros or other currencies. For example:
1.945: mille-neuf-cent-quarante-cinq
1.945 euros: mille neuf cent quarante-cinq euros

When counting above one million, *millions* and *millards* always take an "s" when used in plural. Also notice that you need to put *un* in front of *million* or *milliard* when they're singular.

#	French	English
1.000.000	un-million	one million
2.000.000	deux-millions	two million
4.400.099	quatre-millions-quatre-cent-mille-quatre-vingt-dix-neuf	four million four hundred thousand and ninety-nine
1.000.000.000	un-milliard	one billion
3.000.000.000	trois-milliards	three billion

Pronunciation Tips

- Consonants at the end of *cinq*, *six*, *huit*, and *dix* are not pronounced when followed by a word that begins with a consonant, for example, when saying *cinq-mille* or *dix-millions*.
- When saying a long number, you can pause to take a breath at any separator such as *mille*, *million*, or *milliard*.

Ordinal Numbers

As we mentioned above, ordinal numbers denote the rank, position, or order of items in a group or list, whether that group is made up of people, objects, or things to do.

Examples:
- *Julie est en deuxième position et Marie en cinquième* - Julie is in second place and Marie is in fifth.
- *En premier lieu, il faut laver les légumes* - First, we need to wash the

vegetables.

Once you have familiarized yourself with the cardinal numbers in French, learning the ordinal numbers is a lot easier. You just need to keep a few things in mind.

Ordinal numbers in French are derived from their corresponding number, except for "one," which is *premier*. For the rest, you have to put together the cardinal number and the suffix "-ième."

When the cardinal number ends in "e," the letter disappears to form the ordinal number; i.e. *quatre* becomes *quatrième*. *Cinq* takes an extra "u" at the end (*cinquième*), and the "f" in *neuf* becomes a "v" (*neuvième*).

Keep in mind that *premier* is the only ordinal number that changes to agree in gender and number with the noun it modifies. For instance: *la première idée* - the first idea (*idée* is a feminine and singular noun); *les premiers colonisateurs* - the first colonizers (*colonisateurs* is a masculine and plural noun).

FR Abbreviation	French	EN Abbreviation	English
1er / 1re	premier/première	1st	first
2^{e}	deuxième	2nd	second
3^{e}	troisième	3rd	third
4^{e}	quatrième	4th	fourth
5^{e}	cinquième	5th	fifth
6^{e}	sixième	6th	sixth
7^{e}	septième	7th	seventh
8^{e}	huitième	8th	eighth
9^{e}	neuvième	9th	ninth
10^{e}	dixième	10th	tenth
11^{e}	onzième	11th	eleventh
12^{e}	douzième	12th	twelfth
13^{e}	treizième	13th	thirteenth
14^{e}	quatorzième	14th	fourteenth

15ᵉ	quinzième	15th	fifteenth
16ᵉ	seizième	16th	sixteenth
17ᵉ	dix-septième	17th	seventeenth
18ᵉ	dix-huitième	18th	eighteenth
19ᵉ	dix-neuvième	19th	nineteenth
20ᵉ	vingtième	20th	twentieth
21ᵉ	vingt-et-unième	21st	twenty-first
22ᵉ	vingt-deuxième	22nd	twenty-second
50ᵉ	cinquantième	50th	fiftieth
100ᵉ	centième	100th	hundredth

Using French Numbers in Context

As we mentioned at the beginning of this chapter, numbers in French are used in particular situations to talk about quantity, prices, date and time, age, phone numbers, as well as many other things. When learning the numbers, it's important to learn the expressions and structures in which we might find them as well.

In the following subsections, we will go through the most useful and common contexts and situations where numbers are used.

<u>Dates</u>

In French, cardinal numbers are used to express the date, except for the first day of the month, where the ordinal number *premier* is used instead. In addition, unlike English, French uses a different format where the order of the day and month are reversed.

Here are a few examples:

01/03/2015 – Le 1ᵉʳ mars 2015
02/08/1998 – Le 2 août 1998
28/04/2020 – Le 28 avril 2020

To ask someone the date, we say:
Quelle est la date aujourd'hui ? / What is the date today?

There are several ways to answer that question:
- C'est + le + number + month + year. C'est le 12 juillet 2019 / It's July 12th, 2019.
- Nous sommes + le + number + month + year. Nous sommes le 26 novembre 1996 / It's November 26th, 1996.
- On est + le + number + month + year. On est le 1er janvier 2022 / It's January 1st, 2022.

To include the day of the week with the date, use the following format:
C'est / nous sommes / on est + day of the week + le + number + month + year
C'est samedi, le 16 mai 2011. It's Saturday, May 16th, 2011
On est mardi, le 4 octobre, 2013. It's Tuesday, October 4th, 2013.

Notice that, in French, the days of the week and the months of the year are not capitalized, unlike English.

Bonus!

Increase your vocabulary by learning the days of the week and months of the year in French.

To easily memorize the days of the week, think about our solar system:

Days of the week		
lundi	la Lune	Monday
mardi	Mars	Tuesday
mercredi	Mercure	Wednesday
jeudi	Jupiter	Thursday
vendredi	Vénus	Friday
samedi	Saturne	Saturday
dimanche		Sunday

Months of the year	
janvier	January
février	February
mars	March
avril	April
mai	May
juin	June
juillet	July
août	August
septembre	September
octobre	October
novembre	November
décembre	December

Telling the time

There are two ways of expressing time in French, either with the 12-hour or the 24-hour system; the former is the most common. In either case, we use cardinal numbers to tell the time.

Ways of asking for the time:
Quelle heure est-il ? / What time is it?
Il est quelle heure ? / What time is it?
Est-ce que vous avez l'heure, s'il vous plaît ? / Do you have the time, please?

To answer, follow the format:
Il est + number + heure(s)
Il est une heure (1h00) / It's one o'clock (1 am)
Il est seize heures trente (16h30) / It's four thirty (4:30 pm)

To abbreviate a time in French, use the letter "h" (for heure) between the hour and minutes instead of a colon, like in English. Example: 8h10 / 8:10.

Here are a few useful French vocabulary words related to time:

French	English
l'heure	time
midi	noon
minuit	midnight
et quart	and a quarter
moins le quart	quarter to
et demie	and a half
du matin	in the morning
de l'après-midi	in the afternoon
du soir	in the evening

Examples:
- Il est deux heures / It's two o'clock (2am)
- Il est quatre heures cinq / It's five past four (4:05am)
- Il est quatre heures et quart / It's a quarter past four (4:15am)
- Il est trois heures et demie - Il est trois heures trente / It's half past three - It's three thirty (3:30 am)
- Il est midi / It's noon
- Il est midi cinq (12h05) / It's five past twelve (12:05pm)
- Il est minuit / It's midnight
- Il est minuit moins dix / It's ten minutes to midnight (11:50pm)
- Il est quatre heures moins vingt de l'après-midi / It's twenty minutes to four (3:40pm)
- Il est huit heures moins le quart du soir / It's a quarter to eight (7:45pm)
- Il est sept heures du matin / It's seven in the morning
- Il est huit heures du soir / It's eight o'clock in the evening

Bonus!

Now that you know the basics for telling the time in French, expand your vocabulary by studying some words related to divisions of time as well as parts of the day.

Divisions of time	
une seconde	a second
une minute	a minute
une heure	an hour
un jour, une journée	a day / a whole day
une semaine	a week
un mois	a month
un an, une année	a year / a whole year
une décennie	a decade
un siècle	a century
un millénaire	a millennium

Parts of the day	
le lever du soleil	sunrise
l'aube (f)	dawn
le matin	morning
l'après-midi (m)	afternoon
midi (m)	noon
le soir	evening
le crépuscule	dusk
le coucher du soleil	sunset
la nuit	night
minuit (m)	midnight

Grammar Bonus: "Tu" vs. "Vous"

The distinction between the pronouns *tu* and *vous* is one of the most basic aspects when learning French. Both words mean "you" in English, so choosing one can sometimes be a bit confusing.

In a nutshell, *tu* is informal and singular, while *vous* is formal and singular or plural.

	Informal	Formal
Singular	tu	vous
Plural	vous	vous

It's only when talking to a single person that the choice between *tu* and *vous* must be made.

When addressing people, the degree of closeness between the speakers as well as the situation in which they are speaking would require choosing one or the other.
- *Tu* is used when you are speaking to someone familiar, someone you have a close relationship with (friends, family, relatives, colleagues, classmates), or people within the same age group or younger than you are. *Tu* is also used when talking to God, children, animals, or inanimate objects.
- *Vous* is used for addressing people in a respectful and/or distant way, such as strangers, people with higher authority than you, people older than you, and in professional and academic hierarchies (boss-employee and professor-student relationships). In other words, the pronoun *vous* is the polite way to address someone you do not know well.

Saying your age

The first thing you need to know when talking about someone's age in French is that you use the verb *avoir* (to have), instead of *être* (to be), to structure the sentence; i.e. in English we say "I am five years old" whereas in French you would say "I have five years old." For example: *Il a cinq ans* (he is five years old).

To ask someone's age, you can say:
- Quel âge avez-vous ? (formal) - Quel âge as-tu ? (informal) / How old are you ?
- Quel âge a-t-il ? - (formal) / How old is he?
- Elle a quel âge ? - (informal) / How old is she?

To answer, use the following format: pronoun/noun + verb *avoir* + number of years + *ans*:

- J'ai 65 ans / I'm 65 (years old)
- Elle a 13 ans / She's 13 (years old)
- Les élèves ont 10 ans / The students are 10 (years old)

If you want to know when the birthday of someone is, then ask:
- Quand est ton anniversaire ? / Quand est votre anniversaire ? / When is your birthday?
- Mon anniversaire c'est le vingt-et-un juillet / My birthday is on July 21st

If you want to ask somebody the year when they were born, use the following expression:
- Quand êtes-vous né(e) ? (formal) - Quand es-tu né(e) ? (informal) / When were you born?
- Je suis né(e) en 1997 / I was born in 1997
- Je suis né(e) le 12 octobre 2001 / I was born on October 12, 2001

Pronunciation Tip

For years between 1100 and 1999, there are two equally valid ways of pronunciation:
- Pronounce it like a regular number:
    » 1997: mille-neuf-cent-quatre-vingt-dix-sept
    » 1865: mille-huit-cent-soixante-cinq
- Use the *centaines vigésimales* counting system, that is, break the year into two pairs of two-digit numbers, and place the word "cent" between the pairs:
    » 1997: dix-neuf-cent-quatre-vingt-dix-sept
    » 1865: dix-huit-cent-soixante-cinq

> **Cultural Fact**
>
> Did you know that the French believe that flowers should only be given in odd numbers?
>
> According to French traditions, an odd number of stems mean good luck, except for the number 13, which is considered unlucky no matter the situation. On the other hand, an even number of flowers are reserved for grieving and funerals.

Phone numbers

In general, French speakers give their phone number in chunks of two digits at a time. Numbers in the US, for example, are given as a three-digit area code, followed by three digits, then the other four with pauses (–) in between. In French, phone numbers are written in two-digit chunks and pronounced as two-digit numbers.

US: (012) 345-6789
Pronounced: zero one two – three four five – six seven eight nine.

France: 01 23 45 67 89
Pronounced: zéro un – vingt-trois – quarante-cinq – soixante-sept – quatre-vingt-neuf.

To ask someone their phone number, simply say:
Quel est ton numéro de téléphone ? (informal) - Quel est votre numéro de téléphone ? (formal) / What is your telephone number?

And to answer, just say:
Mon numéro de téléphone est le 05 55 55 55 55 / My telephone number is 05 55 55 55 55.

Prices

To ask how much something costs, say:

Combien ça coûte ? / How much is it?

Now, if you want to ask how much a specific item is, you must replace the "ça" by "ce" before a masculine noun or "cette" before a feminine noun.

Examples:
Combien coûte ce livre ? / How much is that book?
Combien coûte cette voiture ? / How much is that car?

To answer, use any of the following ways:
Ça coûte 40 euros / It costs 40 euros.
Ça fait 68 euros / It's 68 euros.
C'est 780 euros / It's 780 euros.

Alternatively, you can place the noun at the beginning and omit "ça":
L'armoire coûte 200 euros / The cupboard costs 200 euros.

Useful tips when talking about prices:

- In French, the currency symbol comes after the number, unlike English where it's placed before the number. For example:
  » English: $ 10 / € 28
  » French: 10 $ / 28 €
- Decimal numbers in French are separated by a comma (une virgule) while in English a period or full stop is used. Example:
  » English: It costs 28.99 euros
  » French: Ça coûte 28,99 euros

Approximate numbers

In English, we often use expressions like "around" or "about" to make a quick guess about quantities of people, things, items, etc. For instance: There are around thirty students in the class. There are about a thousand chairs in the room.

In French, you can build these words by adding the suffix "-aine" to the number. For example:
une dizaine (about ten)

une quinzaine (about fifteen)
une vingtaine (about twenty)
une centaine (about one hundred)

Here's how you would use them in a sentence:
Il y a une trentaine d'étudiants dans la classe / There are around thirty students in the class.
Il y a une centaine de chaises dans la salle / There are about a hundred chairs in the room.

Using ordinal numbers

As you may have noticed, cardinal numbers are used in most contexts, however, there are some instances when ordinal numbers are handy (besides their core use which is denoting the rank, position, or order of items in a group or list):

- To tell the floor number or the district number when giving an address:
    » J'habite au sixième étage / I live on the sixth floor.
    » J'habite entre les deuxième et troisième arrondissements de Marseille / I live between the second and third districts of Marseille.
- To talk about centuries:
    » Le 21e siècle (pronounced as vingt-et-unième siècle) / 21st century
- To tell fractions:
    » 1/8 = un huitième / an eighth
    » 2/5 = deux cinquièmes / two fifths
- To tell the date, but only for the 1st day of the month:
    » Le premier mai / 1st May

Cultural Fact

Did you know that if you are on the "first floor" in France, it actually means you are on a second floor in America?

Well, it turns out that in France, as well as in most other European countries, floors are a number lower than in the US because they don't count the ground floor of a building when numbering its storeys. So in France, you will find the *rez-de-chaussée* first, or ground floor (equivalent to the first floor for Americans), and then *le premier étage* (which literally translates to first floor but means second floor for Americans).

If you happen to be in Quebec, then don't worry about removing floor numbers as French-Canadian speakers implement the same system as the US.

Bonus 1: Top 101 French words

Here is a list of the 101 most used words in French. In the next section, we'll define each word as well as give examples.

1. le	35. où	69. comment	
2. de	36. si	70. chaque	
3. un	37. bien	71. ensemble	
4. je	38. petit	72. maison	
5. à	39. même	73. grand	
6. et	40. elle	74. ici	
7. en	41. entre	75. pourquoi	
8. était	42. celui	76. gens	
9. eu	43. aussi	77. besoin	
10. la	44. très	78. animal	
11. que	45. autre	79. mère	
12. est	46. y	80. près	
13. dans	47. leur	81. travail	
14. sont	48. avant	82. lieu	
15. qui	49. cela	83. seulement	
16. ne	50. encore	84. tous	
17. sur	51. vous	85. dont	
18. pas	52. déjà	86. non	
19. tout	53. mon	87. raison	
20. son	54. premier	88. depuis	
21. peu	55. aucun	89. bon	
22. temps	56. alors	90. lequel	
23. par	57. après	91. heure	
24. avec	58. fois	92. merci	
25. pour	59. moins	93. ils	
26. mais	60. quelque	94. dehors	
27. chose	61. notre	95. vie	
28. jour	62. an	96. ami	
29. plus	63. personne	97. mot	
30. ce	64. part	98. femme	
31. les	65. dernier	99. monde	
32. il	66. beaucoup	100. monsieur	
33. comme	67. pendant	101. père	
34. on	68. ainsi		

1. le/l': definite article, masculine (the) / pronoun (it)
    - Je veux visiter le musée d'histoire naturelle.
    - I want to visit the museum of natural history. - (article)
    - L'étudiant n'est pas venu au cours.
    - The student didn't come to class. - (article)
    - Je le trouve amusant ce film, pas toi ?
    - I find it funny this film, don't you? - (pronoun)

2. de: preposition (of, from)
    - C'est une cousine de ma mère.
    - She's a cousin of my mother
    - Mon ami vient de Lyon.
    - My friend comes from Lyon.
    - Ses parents travaillent de 6 h à 14 h.
    - Their parents work from 6 am to 2 pm.

3. un: indefinite article, masculin, (a, an)
    - J'ai un chien trop mignon.
    - I have a cute dog.
    - Je voudrais un café s'il vous plaît.
    - I would like a coffee please.
    - Elle a rencontré un ami l'autre jour.
    - She met a friend the other day.

4. je: pronoun (I)
    - Je m'appelle Julian.
    - My name is Julian.
    - J'habite à Paris, près de mon frère.
    - I live in Paris, close to my brother.
    - Je ne connais pas cette fille.
    - I don't know that girl.

5. à: preposition (at, to, in)
    - J'ai vu ma voisine à la poste.
    - I saw my neighbor at the post office.
    - Nous allons à la bibliothèque.
    - We're going to the library.
    - Il habite à Paris maintenant.
    - He lives in Paris now.

6. et: conjunction (and)

- Mon frère <u>et</u> moi partons au ski.
- Ils aiment le café <u>et</u> le thé.
- J'ai tout essayé <u>et</u> je ne sais plus quoi faire.

- My brother and I are going skiing.
- They like coffee and tea.
- I've tried everything and I don't know what to do now.

7. en: preposition (in, of, into)
   - J'ai d'abord vécu <u>en</u> Normandie, puis à Madrid <u>en</u> Espagne.
   - Bien que les nouvelles chaises soient <u>en</u> bois, elles sont très confortables.
   - Le petit garçon a accidentellement brisé le miroir <u>en</u> mille morceaux, heureusement il ne lui est rien arrivé.

   - I lived in Normandy first, then in Madrid in Spain.
   - Although the new chairs are made of wood, they are very comfortable.
   - The little boy accidentally broke the mirror into pieces, fortunately nothing happened to him.

8. était (from the verb être): 3rd person singular, imperfect tense of the indicative (was)
   - La semaine dernière, Anne <u>était</u> malade.
   - Il <u>était</u> sous la douche quand sa mère a appelé.
   - Ce livre <u>était</u> son préféré.

   - Last week Anne was sick.
   - He was in the shower when his mother called.
   - This book was his favorite one.

9. eu (from the verb avoir): past participle (had)
   - À la fête, j'ai <u>eu</u> l'occasion de rencontrer une personne très intéressante.
   - Mon père a <u>eu</u> un mal de tête la nuit dernière.
   - Nous avons <u>eu</u> un bon dîner avec mes parents.

   - At the party, I had the opportunity to meet a very interesting person.
   - My father had a headache last night.
   - We had a lovely dinner with my parents.

10. **la**: definite article, feminine (the) / pronoun (her/it)
    - Tom regarde <u>la</u> télé tous les soirs après le dîner.
    - Tom watches (the) TV every night after dinner. - (article)
    - Marie veut déplacer <u>la</u> table au milieu du salon.
    - Marie wants to move the table to the middle of the living room. - (article)
    - Ma cousine ? Je ne <u>la</u> vois presque jamais, elle habite trop loin.
    - My cousin? I hardly ever see her, she lives too far away. - (pronoun)

11. **que**: pronoun (what, that)
    - <u>Que</u> dis-tu ?
    - What are you saying?
    - Elle ne sait <u>que</u> faire, c'est une situation difficile.
    - She doesn't know what to do, that's a tough situation.
    - Mon oncle pense <u>que</u> tu as raison, mais pas moi.
    - My uncle thinks that you're right but I don't.

12. **est** (from the verb être): 3rd person singular of the present indicative (is)
    - C'<u>est</u> Oliver, mon mari.
    - He is Oliver, my husband.
    - Ma grand-mère <u>est</u> très gentille.
    - My grandmother is very sweet.
    - Il <u>est</u> temps de rentrer à la maison.
    - It's time to go home.

13. **dans**: preposition (in, into, inside)
    - La robe est <u>dans</u> le placard.
    - The dress is in the closet.
    - Il a versé de l'eau <u>dans</u> le verre.
    - He poured water into the glass.
    - Je veux rester <u>dans</u> ma chambre toute la journée.
    - I want to stay inside my room all day.

14. **sont** (from the verb être): 3rd person plural of the present indicative (are)
    - Les garçons là-bas <u>sont</u> allemands.
    - The boys over there are Germans.

- Ces chaussures <u>sont</u> très confortables.
- Les spectacles de ballet et de danse <u>sont</u> mes préférés.

- These shoes are very comfortable.
- Ballet and dancing shows are my favorite.

15. qui: pronoun (who, which, that)
- <u>Qui</u> frappe à la porte ?
- Voici le livre <u>qui</u> était sur mon lit.
- Je vais prendre le train <u>qui</u> va à Rome.

- Who is knocking on the door?
- Here's the book that was on my bed.
- I'm taking the train which is going to Rome.

16. ne/n': adverb (not)
- Je <u>ne</u> mange pas de porc parce que je suis végétarien.
- Ma sœur <u>n</u>'aime pas faire la vaisselle.
- Ils <u>ne</u> veulent pas regarder ce film parce qu'il n'en finit pas.

- I don't eat pork because I'm vegetarian.
- My sister doesn't like to do the dishes.
- They don't want to watch that movie because it lasts forever.

17. sur: preposition (on, about)
- J'ai laissé mes clés <u>sur</u> la table mais maintenant je ne les trouve plus.
- Il est <u>sur</u> quoi ce film ?
- Des feuilles d'arbres flottent <u>sur</u> la piscine.

- I left my keys on the table but now I can't find them.
- What is that film about?
- Some tree leaves are floating on the swimming pool.

18. pas: adverb (not)
- Les résultats du pôle ne sont <u>pas</u> positifs.
- Clara ne peut <u>pas</u> danser, elle a deux pieds gauches.
- Ne <u>pas</u> déranger s'il vous plaît !

- The results from the pole are not positive.
- Clara can't dance, she has two left feet.
- Please, do not disturb!

19. tout: pronoun / adjective (everything, all of, all)
   - Je ferai <u>tout</u> ce que je peux pour te revoir.
   - I will do everything I can to see you again. - (pronoun)
   - Tu as mangé <u>tout</u> ton sandwich ?
   - Did you eat all your sandwich? - (adjective)
   - Martin a dépensé <u>toutes</u> ses économies.
   - Martin has spent all of his savings. - (adjective)

20. son: possessive adjective (his, her, its)
   - Ma femme est très proche de <u>son</u> frère.
   - My wife is very close to her brother.
   - Le chaton joue avec <u>son</u> jouet.
   - The kitten plays with its toy.
   - J'apprécie vraiment <u>son</u> opinion sur le sujet.
   - I really appreciate her opinion on the subject.

21. peu: adverb (not much, little, a little, a bit, few)
   - Il y a <u>peu</u> d'espace entre cette table et le mur.
   - There is little space between that table and the wall.
   - Roxane parle espagnol et un <u>peu</u> français.
   - Roxane speaks Spanish and a bit of French.
   - <u>Peu</u> de gens connaissent la sculptrice Camille Claudel.
   - Few people know of the sculptor Camille Claudel.

22. temps: noun (time)
   - Le <u>temps</u> passe vite quand on s'amuse !
   - Time flies when you're having fun!
   - Nous n'avons pas le <u>temps</u> d'accomplir cette tâche aujourd'hui.
   - We don't have time to complete this task today.
   - Pendant mon <u>temps</u> libre, j'aime tricoter.
   - In my free time, I love to knit.

23. par: preposition (by, through, per)
   - La lettre a été signée <u>par</u> les deux enfants.
   - The letter was signed by both children.

- Le train passe <u>par</u> une petite partie de la forêt.
- Il y a deux types de desserts <u>par</u> personne.

- The train passes through a small part of the forest.
- There are two types of desserts per person.

24. avec: preposition (with)
- Vincent est venu à la fête <u>avec</u> ses amis.
- Je ne veux plus être <u>avec</u> toi.
- J'ai accidentellement cassé la lampe <u>avec</u> ma jambe.

- Vincent came to the party with his friends.
- I don't want to be with you anymore.
- I accidentally broke the lamp with my leg.

25. pour: preposition (to, for, in order to)
- Il me faut une heure <u>pour</u> me préparer.
- Monique a acheté un cadeau <u>pour</u> son fils.
- Il travaille dur <u>pour</u> aller à l'université.

- It takes me one hour to get ready.
- Monique bought a gift for her son.
- He works hard in order to go to college.

26. mais: conjunction (but)
- Je suis fatigué, <u>mais</u> je vais quand même aller à la fête.
- Ce gâteau n'a pas l'air bon, <u>mais</u> il a si bon goût.
- Alice est allée à la banque, <u>mais</u> elle était déjà fermée.

- I feel tired, but I'll go to the party anyway.
- This cake doesn't look good, but it tastes so well.
- Alice went to the bank, but it was already closed.

27. chose: noun, feminine (thing)
- Vous devez vous concentrer sur la <u>chose</u> la plus importante.
- J'ai trouvé de jolies <u>choses</u> dans cette boutique.

- You have to focus on the most important thing.
- I found some lovely things in this shop.

- J'ai tellement de <u>choses</u> en tête en ce moment.
- I have so many things in my head right now.

28. jour: noun, masculine (day)
    - Un <u>jour</u>, j'irai te rendre visite en Espagne.
    - One day I will go to visit you in Spain.
    - Dans deux <u>jours</u>, je vais à la plage.
    - In two days, I'm going to the beach.
    - Le <u>jour</u> où elle est arrivée, il neigeait.
    - The day she came in, it snowed.

29. plus: adverb (more, no more, no longer)
    - Nous avons besoin de <u>plus</u> d'argent pour réaliser le projet.
    - We need more money to accomplish the project.
    - Je n'ai <u>plus</u> d'idées, j'abandonne.
    - I have no more ideas, I give up.
    - Ils ne peuvent <u>plus</u> attendre, ils doivent partir.
    - They can no longer wait, they have to go.

30. ce/c': pronoun / adjective (this, that, it)
    - <u>Ce</u> roman est super intéressant.
    - That novel is super interesting. - (adjective)
    - <u>Ce</u> mot indique le contraire.
    - This word indicates the opposite. - (adjective)
    - <u>C</u>'est une situation difficile pour tout le monde.
    - It's a difficult situation for everyone. - (pronoun)

31. les: definite article, plural (the) / pronoun (them)
    - J'ai entendu la sonnette, je pense que <u>les</u> invités sont arrivés.
    - I heard the doorbell, I think the guests have arrived. - (article)
    - Veuillez classer <u>les</u> livres par ordre alphabétique.
    - Please organize the books in alphabetical order. - (article)
    - Mes amis sont arrivés tard hier soir. Je <u>les</u> ai entendus arriver.
    - My friends arrived late last night. I heard them arrive. - (pronoun)

32. il: pronoun, third person, singular, masculine (he) / impersonal, singular (it)

- Jacques est venu me voir pendant que j'étais malade. <u>Il</u> m'a apporté des fleurs.
- Jacques came to see me while I was sick in bed. He brought me flowers.
- Victor est allé au centre commercial et a acheté un nouveau vélo pour sa femme ; <u>il</u> est violet.
- Victor went to the shopping mall and bought a new bike for his wife; it's purple.
- <u>Il</u> est important de lire attentivement les instructions avant de démarrer l'appareil.
- It's important to read carefully the instructions before starting the device.

33. comme: conjunction (like, as, how)

- <u>Comme</u> toi, j'aime beaucoup jouer du piano.
- Like you, I enjoy playing the piano a lot.
- Antoine travaille <u>comme</u> professeur de mathématiques dans mon école.
- Antoine works as a math teacher in my school.
- <u>Comme</u> tu es belle aujourd'hui !
- How beautiful you look today!

34. on: pronoun, singular (you, we, somebody/someone)

- <u>On</u> ne sait jamais quoi faire quand on est confronté à ce genre de problèmes.
- You never know what to do when confronted with these kinds of problems.
- <u>On</u> est en retard pour le congrès à cause de la circulation.
- We are late for the congress because of the traffic.
- <u>On</u> vous demande à la réception de l'hôtel.
- Someone is asking for you at the hotel reception.

35. où: adverb / conjunction (where)

- <u>Où</u> voulez-vous aller pour le dîner ?
- Where do you want to go for dinner? - (adverb)
- <u>Où</u> est mon portefeuille ? Je ne le trouve pas !
- Where is my wallet? I can't find it! - (adverb)

- La maison <u>où</u> habite Lisa est la plus ancienne du quartier.
- The house where Lisa lives is the oldest one in the neighborhood.- (conjunction)

36. si: conjunction (if)
    - <u>Si</u> vous ne venez pas à la réunion, veuillez nous en informer à l'avance.
    - If you are not coming to the meeting, please let us know in advance.
    - <u>Si</u> les enfants ont faim, ils peuvent manger ces sandwichs.
    - If they kids get hungry, they can eat these sandwiches.
    - On peut aller au cinéma ce soir <u>si</u> le temps le permet.
    - We can go to the movies tonight if the weather is good.

37. bien: adverb / adjective (well, correctly, good)
    - Elle parle <u>bien</u> l'italien ; elle prend des cours particuliers depuis un an.
    - She speaks Italian well; she has been taking personal lessons for the last year. - (adverb)
    - Êtes-vous sûr d'avoir <u>bien</u> compris les instructions ?
    - Are you sure you understood the instructions correctly? - (adverb)
    - C'est très <u>bien</u> comme ça.
    - It's very good like that. - (adjective)

38. petit: adjective (small, short, little)
    - Nous dormons dans un <u>petit</u> lit ; je pense qu'il est temps d'en prendre un plus grand.
    - We sleep on a small bed; I think it's time to get a bigger one.
    - Mon grand frère est si <u>petit</u>, mais il n'a que 9 ans.
    - My big brother is so short, but he's only 9 years old.
    - Ma petite amie est pleine de <u>petites</u> attentions pour moi.
    - My girlfriend is always doing little things for me.

39. même: adjective / adverb (same, the same, even)
    - Les deux filles conduisent la <u>même</u> voiture.
    - The two girls drive the same car. - (adjective)

- Nous avons adoré le pain à l'avoine de la nouvelle boulangerie, achète le <u>même</u> s'il-te-plaît.
- We loved the oat bread from the new bakery, please get the same. - (adjective)
- Ce n'est pas facile de vivre dans une ville aussi chère, <u>même</u> pour moi.
- It's not easy to live in such an expensive city, even for me. - (adverb)

40. elle: pronoun, third person, singular, feminine (she) / impersonal, singular (it)
- Emma aime tous les sports ; <u>elle</u> aime particulièrement jouer au tennis.
- Emma loves all sports; she especially enjoys playing tennis.
- Que pense-t-<u>elle</u> de votre décision ?
- What does she think about your decision?
- J'ai acheté une nouvelle robe pour le mariage de ma sœur ; <u>elle</u> est rouge.
- I bought a new dress for my sister's wedding; it's red.

41. entre: preposition (between, amongst)
- Robert a garé son vélo <u>entre</u> deux voitures.
- Robert parked his bike between two cars.
- J'admire la grande énergie <u>entre</u> les adversaires.
- I admire the great energy between the opponents.
- <u>Entre</u> toutes ces fleurs, ce sont celles-ci que je préfère.
- Amongst all these flowers, these are the ones I prefer.

42. celui: demonstrative pronoun (the one, he)
- Ce roman historique est <u>celui</u> que tu avais tant aimé.
- This historical novel is the one you liked so much.
- Ce ballon est <u>celui</u> que j'ai trouvé dehors sur le sol.
- This ball is the one I found outside on the floor.
- <u>Celui</u> qui mange bien travaille bien.
- He who eats well works well.

43. aussi: adverb (too, also, as well)
- Gina aime la musique classique, mais elle apprécie <u>aussi</u> la musique reggae et le soft rock.
- Gina loves classical music, but she enjoys reggae music and soft rock too.
- J'ai deux frères et <u>aussi</u> une sœur.
- I have two brothers and also a sister.
- Nous prévoyons un voyage pour aller skier, voulez-vous venir <u>aussi</u> ?
- We're planning a trip to go skiing, would you like to come as well?

44. très: adverb (very)
- Sarah est <u>très</u> fatiguée ce matin car elle a dû marcher jusqu'à son travail après avoir manqué le bus.
- Sarah is very tired this morning because she had to walk all the way to her work after missing the bus.
- Il est <u>très</u> important de se souvenir de mon conseil quand vous parlez à votre patron.
- It's very important to remember my advice when talking to your boss.
- Elle parle déjà trois langues ; c'est une femme <u>très</u> intelligente.
- She already speaks three languages; she is a very intelligent woman.

45. autre: adjective (another, other)
- Mon verre est vide et le vôtre aussi, voulez-vous un <u>autre</u> verre ?
- My glass is empty and yours too, do you want another drink?
- Pense à une <u>autre</u> solution, les choses doivent changer bientôt.
- Think about another solution, things need to change soon.
- L'homme vendait de la limonade, du coca et d'<u>autres</u> boissons dans la rue.
- The man was selling lemonade, coke, and other drinks in the street.

46. y: adverb / pronoun (there, it)
- Nous partons maintenant pour le centre commercial. Alice nous <u>y</u> attend.
- We're leaving now to the shopping mall. Alice is waiting for us there. - (adverb)

- Cette erreur sera bientôt corrigée par notre équipe technique, vous pouvez <u>y</u> compter.
- J'ai hâte de retourner en France. J'<u>y</u> étais l'année dernière.

- This error will be fixed soon by our tech team, you can count on it. - (pronoun)
- I can't wait to go back to France. I was there last year. - (adverb)

47. leur: possessive adjective (their)

- Les garçons aiment beaucoup <u>leur</u> animal de compagnie, Murry, une petite tortue.
- Je me fiche de <u>leur</u> opinion, je fais ça à ma façon.
- Paul et Anne forment un couple charmant, mais ces derniers temps, les problèmes affectent gravement <u>leur</u> relation.

- The boys love so much their pet, Murry, a little turtle.
- I don't care about their opinion, I'm doing this my way.
- Paul and Anne make a lovely couple, but lately problems are affecting badly their relationship.

48. avant: preposition (before)

- Je dois prendre une douche <u>avant</u> d'aller chez le médecin.
- Les enfants ont déjeuné <u>avant</u> midi, ils avaient trop faim.
- <u>Avant</u> de partir tous les deux, faites la vaisselle s'il vous plaît.

- I need to take a shower before going to the doctor.
- The kids had lunch before noon, they were too hungry.
- Before you two leave, please do the dishes.

49. cela: pronoun (that)

- C'était très agréable, mais <u>cela</u> n'a pas fait de différence pour eux.
- J'ai vraiment apprécié ma conversation avec Karine ; <u>cela</u> m'a soulagée.
- <u>Cela</u> ne veut pas dire qu'on doit partir maintenant, n'est-ce pas ?

- That was very pleasant, but that didn't make any difference for them.
- I really enjoyed my conversation with Karine; that made me feel relieved.
- That doesn't mean we need to leave right now, does it?

50. encore: adverb (still, yet, more, again)
- Nous sommes tous prêts à partir mais Clair est <u>encore</u> dans le bain.
- We are all ready to leave but Clair is still in the bathroom.
- Je travaille aussi vite que je peux, mais je n'ai pas <u>encore</u> terminé.
- I am working as fast as I can but I have not yet finished yet.
- Tu as fini ton pain. Tu en veux <u>encore</u> ?
- You have finished your bread. Do you want some more?

51. vous: pronoun, second person, singular/plural (you)
- Et <u>vous</u>, M. Smith, d'où venez-<u>vous</u> ?
- And you Mr. Smith, where do you come from?
- <u>Vous</u>, les enfants, vous me rendez folle aujourd'hui, arrêtez s'il vous plaît.
- You, kids, you're driving me crazy today, please stop.
- <u>Vous</u> devez essayer ce vin, Maurice l'a ramené de son dernier voyage en Europe.
- You need to try this wine, Maurice brought it from his last trip to Europe.

52. déjà: adverb (already, yet)
- Quand mes parents sont rentrés, j'étais <u>déjà</u> parti au travail.
- When my parents got home, I had already left to work.
- Tu as <u>déjà</u> remarqué que Sam n'était pas là ?
- Did you already notice that Sam isn't here?
- Mark a <u>déjà</u> dîné dans le nouveau restaurant, il a dit que son plat était splendide.
- Mark already had dinner at the new restaurant, he said his dish was splendid.

53. mon: possessive adjective (my)
- <u>Mon</u> numéro de téléphone est le 78 58 52 41.
- My telephone number is 78 58 52 41.
- Demain, c'est <u>mon</u> anniversaire, nous avons prévu de dîner chez Clara. Voulez-vous venir ?
- Tomorrow is my birthday, we're planning to have dinner at Clara's place. Would you like to come?

- <u>Mon</u> nouvel appartement est beaucoup plus confortable que l'ancien, mais plus éloigné de la ville.
- My new apartment is much more comfortable than the old one, but more distant from town.

54. premier: adjective (first)

- C'est la <u>première</u> fois que je voyage seule, et c'est une excellente expérience jusqu'à présent.
- This is the first time I travel on my own, it has been a great experience so far.
- Le <u>premier</u> examen de Marie ne s'est pas bien passé, elle est toute bouleversée dans sa chambre.
- Marie's first exam didn't go well, she is all upset in her room.
- La <u>première</u> fois que je l'ai vu, il portait un pull bleu et un pantalon de sport blanc.
- The first time I saw him he was wearing a blue sweater and white sport pants.

55. aucun: pronoun (no one, none, neither)

- <u>Aucun</u> de mes amis n'est venu à ma fête à cause de la tempête.
- None of my friends came to my party because of the storm.
- <u>Aucun</u> de nous n'avait envie d'étudier ce matin.
- Neither of us felt like studying this morning.
- <u>Aucune</u> des personnes présentes dans la pièce n'a dit quoi que ce soit à l'homme en colère.
- None of the people in the room said anything to the angry man.

56. alors: adverb (then, so)

- Si tu es libre ce week-end, <u>alors</u> tu devrais rendre visite à tes parents à la maison de retraite.
- If you're free this weekend, then you should visit your parents at the nursing home.
- <u>Alors</u>, raconte-moi ce qui s'est passé hier soir, n'oublie aucun détail !
- So, tell me what happened last night, don't miss any detail!
- Nous avons de gros problèmes, qu'allons-nous faire <u>alors</u> ?
- We're in big trouble, what are we going to do then?

57. après: preposition (after)
- <u>Après</u> avoir quitté son emploi, elle a créé sa propre entreprise à domicile.
- After she quit her job, she started her own business at home.
- Notre maison se trouve dans la deuxième rue, <u>après</u> le court de tennis.
- Our house is on the second street, after the tennis court.
- Tu veux aller boire un verre <u>après</u> le cours ?
- Do you want to go for a drink after the class?

58. fois: noun, feminine (time)
- Je suis allé chez le médecin, il m'a recommandé de prendre ce médicament quatre <u>fois</u> par jour.
- I went to the doctor, he recommended me to take this medication four times a day.
- Il est conseillé de manger au moins trois <u>fois</u> par jour.
- It's advisable to eat at least three times a day.
- Jim a manqué le bus plusieurs <u>fois</u> ce mois-ci, il devrait se lever tôt le matin.
- Jim has missed the bus several times this month, he should wake up early in the morning.

59. moins: adverb (less)
- Il est <u>moins</u> attirant quand il se comporte de cette façon.
- He's less attractive when he behaves in such a way.
- Avec ces deux emplois, j'ai plus d'argent mais <u>moins</u> de temps pour moi.
- With these two jobs, I have more money but less time for myself.
- Cet équipement est <u>moins</u> difficile à utiliser que l'autre que nous avions.
- This equipment is less difficult to operate than the other one we had.

60. quelque: adjective (some, certain, about)
- J'ai <u>quelques</u> doutes sur ce rapport, puis-je revoir les résultats ?
- I have some doubts about this report, may I see the results again?

65

- Ils ont eu <u>quelque</u> difficulté avec leur voiture ce matin, alors ils ont décidé de prendre le train.
- Il va y avoir <u>quelque</u> 100 invités à leur mariage.

- They had a certain issue with their car this morning, so they decided to take the train.
- There's going to be about 100 guests at their wedding.

61. notre: possessive adjective (our)
- <u>Notre</u> pays est confronté à de grandes questions politiques en ce moment.
- Patrick et moi travaillons sur <u>notre</u> relation, nous voyons un thérapeute de couple tous les vendredis.
- <u>Notre</u> équipe de basket-ball est la meilleure de la région ; nous avons remporté tous les championnats au cours des cinq dernières années.

- Our country is facing big political issues right now.
- Patrick and I are working on our relationship, we're seeing a couple's therapist every Friday.
- Our basketball team is the best of the region; we have won all championships for the last five years.

62. an: noun, masculine (year, years old)
- Marco a passé quatre <u>ans</u> au Canada et il envisage maintenant de rentrer dans son pays.
- Je pense que Lisa a 20 <u>ans</u>, n'est-ce pas ?
- Fabrice et Clara sont membres du club de golf depuis deux <u>ans</u>.

- Marco has spent four years in Canada and he is now considering moving back to his country.
- I think Lisa is twenty years old, isn't she?
- Fabrice and Clara have been members of the golf club for two years.

63. personne: noun, feminine (person, people –pl)
- Ma grand-mère est une <u>personne</u> serviable et attentionnée ; en effet, elle a travaillé comme infirmière pendant trente ans.

- My grandmother is a helpful and caring person; in fact, she worked as a nurse for thirty years.

- Connaissez-vous cette <u>personne</u>? Celle qui porte un pull noir et un pantalon rouge.
- Il y avait environ 40 <u>personnes</u> à la fête de Charles hier soir.

- Do you know that person? The one wearing a black sweater and red pants.
- There were about 40 people at Charles party last night.

64. part: noun, feminine (part, piece)

- Ils attendent une action de notre <u>part</u>, nous ne pouvons pas les laisser tomber.
- Pouvez-vous couper la pizza en huit <u>parts</u>, s'il vous plaît?
- Camille a mangé une autre <u>part</u> de tarte pour le dîner, maintenant elle a mal au ventre.

- They expect action from our part, we can't let them down.
- Can you please cut the pizza into eight pieces?
- Camille ate another piece of pie for dinner, now she has a stomach ache.

65. dernier: adjective (last, final)

- Le <u>dernier</u> concurrent à arriver était Thomas, il était complètement épuisé.
- L'année <u>dernière</u>, ma famille est allée aux Caraïbes pour les vacances ; cette année, elle ira en Asie.
- Le <u>dernier</u> chapitre de ce livre est le plus mémorable.

- The last competitor to arrive was Thomas, he was completely exhausted.
- Last year, my family went to the Caribbean for holidays; this year they'll go to Asia.
- The final chapter of this book is the most memorable.

66. beaucoup : adverb (a lot, much, many)

- Mon frère aime <u>beaucoup</u> son nouveau travail, il n'arrête pas d'en parler.
- C'est <u>beaucoup</u> mieux de prendre l'autoroute plutôt que la vieille route.

- My brother likes his new job a lot, he doesn't stop talking about it.
- It's much better to take the highway rather than the old road.

- <u>Beaucoup</u> de gens n'ont pas pu venir à la conférence en raison de l'annulation de leur vol.
- Many people couldn't come to the conference due to flight cancellations.

67. pendant: preposition (during, for)
- Je me suis endormi <u>pendant</u> le trajet en train.
- I fell asleep during the train ride.
- Julie a travaillé <u>pendant</u> dix ans dans l'entreprise, au service marketing.
- Julie worked at the company for ten years in the marketing department.
- Léa a étudié l'anglais <u>pendant</u> cinq ans au lycée, mais elle ne sait même pas dire « hi » maintenant.
- Léa studied English for five years at high school, but she can't even say "hi" now.

68. donc: conjunction (so, therefore, hence)
- Vous n'avez pas vu ce qui s'est passé, <u>donc</u> vous ne pouvez rien dire.
- You didn't see what happened, so you can't say anything.
- Cette machine est inutile, nous devons <u>donc</u> remplir ce rapport et en demander une nouvelle.
- This machinery is useless, we therefore need to fill this report and request a new one.
- L'équipe a marqué un but à la toute dernière minute et a <u>donc</u> gagné le match.
- The team scored a goal at the very last minute, thus winning the match.

69. comment: adverb (how)
- <u>Comment</u> avez-vous trouvé le moyen de sortir du bâtiment ?
- How did you find the way out of the building?
- Je sais <u>comment</u> réparer ces appareils, laissez-moi apporter mes outils.
- I know how to repair these devices, let me bring my tools.
- Bonjour Monsieur, <u>comment</u> allez-vous aujourd'hui ?
- Good morning Mister, how are you today?

70. chaque: adjective (each, every)
- Nous allons au cours d'art <u>chaque</u> mercredi, de 9h à 11h.
- We go to art class every Wednesday, from 9am to 11am.
- <u>Chaque</u> personne doit coopérer si nous voulons résoudre ce problème.
- Every person has to cooperate if we want to solve this issue.
- Je suis allé à la nouvelle librairie, ils avaient de bonnes affaires sur les livres classiques. J'en ai acheté cinq, <u>chaque</u> livre m'a coûté environ 8 euros.
- I went to the new bookstore, they had great deals on classic books. I bought five, each book cost me around 8 euros.

71. ensemble: adverb (together) / noun (set, suit)
- Marie et Julian ont dansé toute la nuit <u>ensemble</u>, je pense qu'ils sont amoureux l'un de l'autre.
- Marie and Julian danced all night together, I think they are in love with each other. - (adverb)
- Ce nouvel <u>ensemble</u> lui va très bien.
- This new suit suits looks good on him. - (noun)
- L'entreprise a dû prendre un <u>ensemble</u> de mesures strictes pour éviter la faillite.
- The company had to take a set of strict measures to avoid brankruptcy. - (noun)

72. maison: noun, feminine (house, home)
- Ils possèdent une belle <u>maison</u> à la campagne, près de la forêt.
- They own a beautiful house in the countryside, close to the forest.
- Le dimanche, j'aime rester à la <u>maison</u> et ne faire que manger et dormir.
- On Sundays I like to stay at home and do nothing but eating and sleeping.
- Est-il difficile d'acheter une <u>maison</u> dans ce pays ?
- How difficult is it to get a house in this country?

73. grand: adjective (tall, big, great)
- Même si mes parents sont plutôt petits, mon frère est <u>grand</u>.
- Even though my parents are quite short, my brother is tall.

- Ma chambre dans la nouvelle maison est vraiment <u>grande</u> ; il y a même de la place pour un lit supplémentaire.
- Les <u>grands</u> leaders peuvent influencer les jeunes à agir selon les règles.

- My bedroom at the new house is really big; there is even space for an extra bed.
- Great leaders can influence youth to act according to rules.

74. ici: adverb (here)

- Pourriez-vous entrer et vous asseoir <u>ici</u> ? Je dois vous parler à tous les deux.
- La gare n'est qu'à quelques rues d'<u>ici</u>.
- <u>Ici</u>, dans mon pays, nous portons généralement des vêtements chauds toute l'année.

- Could you please come in and sit down here? I need to talk to both of you.
- The train station is only a few blocks away from here.
- Here, in my country, we usually dress in warm clothes year round.

75. pourquoi: adverb (why)

- <u>Pourquoi</u> viens-tu à la fête habillée comme ça ? Je t'ai dit que c'était une fête formelle.
- Je ne comprends pas <u>pourquoi</u> elle se comporte comme ça.
- <u>Pourquoi</u> le gouvernement a-t-il été si indifférent à l'égard de ceux qui ont perdu leur emploi ?

- Why are you coming to the party dressed like this? I told you it was a formal party.
- I don't understand why she is behaving like that.
- Why has the government been so indifferent to those who have lost their jobs?

76. gens: noun, masculine, plural (people)

- C'est tellement excitant de rencontrer des <u>gens</u> extraordinaires qui changent le monde.
- Chaque jour, les <u>gens</u> trouvent de nouveaux moyens de s'exprimer à travers l'art.

- It's so exciting to meet amazing people who are changing the world.
- Everyday people find new ways to express themselves through art.

- Je ne connais pas ces <u>gens</u> là-bas, je pense que ce sont tous des amis de Marissa.
- I don't know those people over there, I think they are all Marissa's friends.

77. besoin: noun, masculine (need)
- Charles ressent le <u>besoin</u> de fumer une cigarette toutes les heures.
- Charles feels the need to have a cigarette every hour.
- Nous avons <u>besoin</u> de l'autorisation du Conseil de Sécurité pour ce projet.
- We need the authorization of the Security Council for this project.
- J'ai <u>besoin</u> d'un long sommeil ce week-end, ça a été une semaine épuisante.
- I need to take a long sleep this weekend, it's been an exhausting week.

78. animal (animaux in plural): noun, masculine (animal)
- Emily aime tous les <u>animaux</u>, mais elle ne peut pas supporter les cafards.
- Emily loves all animals, but she can't deal with cockroaches.
- J'ai emmené mon enfant au zoo aujourd'hui, il a été émerveillé par les <u>animaux</u> aquatiques qu'il a vus.
- I took my kid to the zoo today, he was amazed by the aquatic animals he saw.
- Le cheval est mon <u>animal</u> préféré.
- Horses are my favorite animal.

79. mère: noun, feminine (mother, mom)
- Ce n'est pas ta <u>mère</u> là-bas ? Elle est si belle ce soir.
- Isn't that your mother over there? She looks so great tonight.
- J'ai eu une longue conversation avec ma <u>mère</u> aujourd'hui, je lui ai parlé de mon intention de déménager.
- I had a long chat with my mom today, I told her about my intention of moving out.
- La jeune fille ressemble beaucoup à sa <u>mère</u>, n'est-ce pas ?
- The young girl looks a lot like her mother, isn't she?

80. près: adverb (near, close)
- Jade habite <u>près</u> de la gare ; malgré cela, elle a raté le train ce matin.
- Jade lives close to the train station; even so, she missed the train this morning.
- Il y a un bar sympa <u>près</u> d'ici ; si tu veux, on peut y aller et boire quelques verres.
- There is a cool bar near here; if you want, we can go there and have some drinks.
- <u>Près</u> de 100 personnes ont signé la demande du gouvernement.
- Close to 100 people have signed the government request.

81. travail: noun, masculine (work, job, task)
- Le <u>travail</u> d'Elaine commence à 9 heures, mais comme aujourd'hui c'est son anniversaire, elle a le droit de prendre un jour de congé.
- Elaine's work begins at 9 o'clock, but because today it's her birthday, she is allowed to take the day off.
- Ce <u>travail</u> requiert des compétences artistiques que je n'ai pas.
- This job requires artistic skills that I don't have.
- Le <u>travail</u> principal aujourd'hui est de terminer le rapport.
- The main task today is to finish the report.

82. lieu: noun, masculine (place, location, spot)
- C'est le <u>lieu</u> où j'aimerais organiser la réception du mariage.
- This is the place where I would like to have the wedding reception.
- La réunion se déroulera en un <u>lieu</u> éloigné, nous vous communiquerons les détails plus tard.
- The meeting is going to take place at a remote location, we'll share the details later on.
- J'aime beaucoup ce <u>lieu</u>, c'est si romantique.
- I love this spot so much, it's so romantic.

83. seulement: adverb (only)
- Il y a <u>seulement</u> deux routes qui mènent à la ferme.
- There are only two roads that lead to the farm.

- Arthur et Sarah ont quatre filles et <u>seulement</u> un fils.
- L'entreprise a besoin d'une solution à long terme, pas <u>seulement</u> d'une solution temporaire.

- Arthur and Sarah have four daughters and only one son.
- The company needs a long-term solution, not just a temporary one.

84. tous: adjective / determinant / pronoun (all, every)

- <u>Tous</u> mes amis sont allés au cinéma, sauf Thiago et Tom.
- Nous devons prendre en compte <u>tous</u> les critères avant de prendre une décision.
- Ils sont <u>tous</u> partis avant la fin du film. C'était un désastre !

- All my friends went to the movies, except Thiago and Tom. - (adjective)
- We need to consider all criteria before making a decision. - (determinant)
- They all left before the end of the film. It was a disaster! - (pronoun)

85. dont: pronoun (whose, of which, of whom)

- C'est un écrivain célèbre et très connu <u>dont</u> j'admire vraiment le travail.
- Ils possèdent deux maisons, <u>dont</u> une au bord de la mer, à côté de la mienne.
- C'est l'ami <u>dont</u> je t'ai parlé, tu te souviens ?

- He is a famous and very well-known writer whose work I truly admire.
- They own two houses, one of which is by the sea, next to mine.
- This is the friend I told you about, remember?

86. non: adverb (no, not)

- Vous devez apprendre à dire oui comme à dire <u>non</u>.
- J'ai trente-neuf ans et <u>non</u> quarante !
- Tu veux venir avec nous ? – <u>Non</u>.

- You need to learn how to say yes as well as no.
- I'm thirty-nine years old, not forty!
- Do you want to come with us? –No.

87. raison: noun, feminine (reason)
- Personne ne connaît la <u>raison</u> de son départ soudain.
- No one knows the reason for his sudden departure.
- Donnez-moi une seule bonne <u>raison</u> de partir et je vous laisserai partir.
- Tell me one good reason to leave and I'll let you go.
- L'accès à cette zone particulière est interdit pour des <u>raisons</u> de sécurité.
- Access to this particular area is forbidden for security reasons.

88. depuis: preposition (since, for, from)
- Notre vie a considérablement changé <u>depuis</u> le départ de notre fils.
- Our life has significantly changed since the departure of our son.
- Nous visitons la même île <u>depuis</u> des années.
- We have visited the same island for years.
- Il y a une belle vue <u>depuis</u> le balcon de ma chambre.
- There is a great view from the balcony of my room.

89. bon: adjective (good, right)
- Je veux emmener Florence dîner, pouvez-vous me recommander un <u>bon</u> restaurant ?
- I want to take Florence for dinner, can you recommend me a good restaurant?
- Ce gâteau est très <u>bon</u>, qui l'a fait ?
- This cake is very good, who made it?
- Vous êtes sûr que c'est le <u>bon</u> bus ?
- Are you sure this is the right bus?

90. lequel: pronoun (which, which one, who)
- <u>Lequel</u> de ces deux cahiers est le tien ?
- Which (one) of these two notebooks is yours?
- C'est la maison d'un homme <u>lequel</u> est mort l'année dernière dans un accident de voiture.
- That was the house of a man who died last year in a car accident.

- J'ai besoin d'un téléphone intelligent, <u>lequel</u> est le moins cher ?
- I need a smartphone, which one is the least expensive?

91. heure: noun, feminine (hour, time)
    - Allez les enfants, c'est l'<u>heure</u> de rentrer à la maison.
    - Come on kids, it's time to go home.
    - Combien d'<u>heures</u> faut-il pour aller de Paris à Lyon en train ?
    - How many hours does it take to go From Paris to Lyon by train?
    - J'ai vu William au centre commercial il y a deux <u>heures</u>, il était avec sa petite amie.
    - I saw William at the mall two hours ago, he was with his girlfriend.

92. merci: interjection / noun masculine (thanks, thank you)
    - Oh, tu m'as apporté des fleurs, <u>merci</u> ! C'est très gentil de ta part.
    - Oh, you brought me flowers, thanks! It's very kind of you.
    - Un grand <u>merci</u> à ma femme, sans son soutien je ne serais pas là.
    - A big thanks for my wife, without her support I wouldn't be here.
    - <u>Merci</u> pour ton aide, maintenant je sais comment utiliser cet outil.
    - Thank you for your help, now I know how to operate this tool.

93. ils: pronoun, third person, plural, masculine (they)
    - Charles et Arthur sont allés au musée, puis <u>ils</u> ont rendu visite à Constance.
    - Charles and Arthur went to the museum, then they visited Constance.
    - Où as-tu mis mes crayons ? - <u>Ils</u> sont sur la table.
    - Where did you put my pencils? - They are on the table.
    - Le professeur a expliqué les différents processus, <u>ils</u> sont faciles à suivre.
    - The teacher explained the different processes, they are easy to follow.

94. dehors: adverb (outside, out, outdoors)

- Le temps est très beau aujourd'hui, alors les enfants jouent <u>dehors</u>.
- Il y a deux hommes qui se battent <u>dehors</u>, on ferait mieux de partir maintenant.
- Faisons un peu d'exercice <u>dehors</u>, j'en ai marre du confinement.

- The weather is very nice today so the kids are playing outside.
- There are two men fighting outside, we better leave now.
- Let's do some exercise outdoors, I'm tired of the lockdown.

95. vie: noun, feminine (life)

- J'ai vécu des expériences particulières qui ont changé ma <u>vie</u>.
- Il a passé toute sa <u>vie</u> à aider les personnes dans le besoin.
- En moyenne, la durée de <u>vie</u> d'une pieuvre peut varier entre 6 mois et 5 ans.

- I have been through some particular experiences that have changed my life.
- He spent his entire life helping those in need.
- On average, the lifespan of an octopus can range between 6 months to 5 years.

96. ami/amie: noun, masculine / feminine (friend, mate)

- J'ai rencontré Armando au lycée, mais nous sommes devenus les meilleurs <u>amis</u> à l'université.
- John aime sortir avec ses <u>amis</u> tous les vendredis après le travail.
- Tu vois ces deux filles dans la voiture rouge ? Ce sont les <u>amies</u> de Mona.

- I met Armando at high school, but we became best friends in college.
- John likes to hang out with his friends every Friday after work.
- Do you see those two girls in the red car? They are Mona's friends.

97. mot : noun, masculine (word)

- Je ne comprends pas le sens de ce <u>mot</u>, je pense que nous devrions en utiliser un autre à la place.

- I don't understand the meaning of this word, I think we should use another one instead.

- Mon père ne veut plus entendre un seul <u>mot</u> sur la fête de Tom.
- My father doesn't want to hear a single word anymore about Tom's party.

- L'auteur a écrit un essai de mille <u>mots</u> sur l'influence de la culture dans les manifestations artistiques.
- The author wrote a thousand word essay about the influence of culture in art manifestations.

98. femme: noun, feminine (woman, wife, lady)
- Aujourd'hui, les <u>femmes</u> sont plus indépendantes et libres de faire ce qu'elles veulent.
- Today, women are more independent and free to do what they want.
- Vous connaissez Christine ? C'est la <u>femme</u> d'Antoine.
- Do you know Christine? She is Antoine's wife.
- Cette <u>femme</u> est absolument superbe dans cette robe rouge et ces talons hauts.
- That lady looks absolutely stunning in that red dress and high heels.

99. monde: noun, masculine (world, planet, crowd)
- Les religions façonnent la conception que les gens ont de leur environnement et du <u>monde</u> en général.
- Religions shape people's conception of their environment and the world in general.
- Le <u>monde</u> subit les conséquences de nos actions, le changement climatique en est un exemple.
- The planet is suffering the consequences of our actions, climate change is an example.
- Il y avait du <u>monde</u> au défilé du carnaval, c'était vraiment amusant et intéressant.
- There was a crowd at the carnival parade, it was really fun and interesting.

100. monsieur: noun, masculine (Mr., gentleman)
- Bienvenue <u>Monsieur</u> Smith, veuillez entrer et vous asseoir où vous voulez.
- Welcome Mister Smith, please come in and have a seat wherever you want.

- <u>Monsieur</u> Durand et sa femme ont pris une tasse de café sur la terrasse de l'hôtel.
- J'ai rencontré un <u>Monsieur</u> charmant et intéressant à l'aéroport aujourd'hui.

- Mr. Durand and his wife had a cup of coffee on the hotel's terrace.
- I met such a charming and interesting gentleman at the airport today.

101. père: noun, masculine (father, dad)

- L'agonie de mon <u>père</u> a été longue et difficile à cause du cancer.
- Nous organisons une fête surprise pour l'anniversaire de mon <u>père</u> ce soir, il n'a aucune idée de ce qui se passe.
- Cet homme est le <u>père</u> de Tim, il a fait un long voyage pour passer Noël avec son fils.

- My father's agony was long and difficult because of the cancer.
- We're having a surprise party for my dad's birthday tonight, he has no idea what is going on.
- That man is Tim's father, he traveled a long way to spend Christmas with his son.

Bonus 2: The Adventures of Clara

Enjoy these two chapters of Clara and her adventures after arriving in France!

Chapitre 1 - Nouvelle vie, nouvelle aventure

Clara est une **jeune** américaine originaire de New York qui vient d'arriver en France, plus précisément à Lyon, où elle va passer un an. Elle s'installe chez Céline Crespo, sa **correspondante** depuis plus d'un an. Clara est un peu **inquiète**, parce que c'est la première fois qu'elle est si **loin** de chez elle et aussi parce qu'elle se sent un peu **préoccupée** par son **niveau** de français. Céline propose de lui présenter ses amis, qui sont très sympas et **accueillants**, et avec qui elle va **pouvoir** pratiquer son français.

Jeune (m, f) (nom commun) : young
Correspondant (m) (adjectif) : penpal
Inquiète (adjectif) : worried
Loin (adverbe) : far

Préoccuper (verbe) : to worry
Niveau (m) (nom commun) : level
Accueillant (adjectif) : welcoming
Pouvoir (verbe) : to be able to

Par chance, c'est le week-end, les amis de Céline sont donc **disponibles** pour se réunir. Ils décident de se retrouver chez Paul, une chaîne de **boulangeries** qui fait de très bonnes pâtisseries. Le **rendez-vous** est à 14h, et il est seulement **midi**, elles ont donc un peu de temps à perdre. Clara pense qu'il serait bien de **faire un** petit **tour** en ville et de prendre le métro, pour **découvrir** son **fonctionnement**. On n'est pas encore en **hiver**, mais il fait vraiment **froid** ce jour-là : elles enfilent des vêtements chauds, mettent leurs **manteaux** et sortent.

Par chance (expression) : luckily
Disponible (adjectif) : available
Boulangerie (f) (nom commun) : bakery
Rendez-vous (m) (nom commun) : meeting
Midi (m) (nom commun) : midday
Faire un tour (expression) : to take a walk
Découvrir (verbe) : to discover
Fonctionnement (m) (nom commun) : the way it works
Hiver (m) (nom commun) : winter
Froid (adjectif) : cold
Manteau (m) (nom commun) : coat

- Ma **maison** est environ à 20 minutes de la station Hôtel de Ville, où on va **retrouver** les copains, explique Céline à Clara. On est à Garibaldi, et on doit changer de métro à Bellecour, qui est au centre-ville.

- **Puisqu'**on a le temps, pourquoi ne pas marcher à partir de Bellecour, comme ça je découvre un peu la ville, propose Clara.

Céline trouve l'idée très bonne, et elles **se mettent en route**.

- Le métro fonctionne très bien à Lyon : il est facile à utiliser, et c'est **quasiment** impossible de **se perdre** ! Par exemple, pour acheter un ticket, tu dois simplement **trouver** une machine, il y en dans toutes les stations, sélectionner le ticket dont tu **as besoin** ce jour-là, et payer par carte ou **en liquide**. Voilà, le ticket s'imprime immédiatement et sera vérifié automatiquement en passant les portillons du métro, explique Céline.

Maison (f) (nom commun) : house
Retrouver (verbe) : to meet
Puisque (conjonction) : since
Se mettre en route (expression) : to set out
Quasiment (adverbe) : almost
Se perdre (verbe) : to get lost
Trouver (verbe) : to find
Avoir besoin (verbe) : to need
En liquide (expression) : by cash

Elles **achètent** toutes les deux leurs tickets et **s'assoient** en attendant l'arrivée du métro. Céline explique à Clara qu'il y a beaucoup de métro qui passent à toute heure, et qu'on n'attend donc **jamais plus** de quelques minutes. C'est l'un des points positifs de ce moyen de transport !

Dans chaque wagon, il y a un panneau qui représente la ligne de métro, comme ça on sait **toujours** quel est le prochain arrêt. **Tant qu'**on y fait attention, on sait toujours **où** on se trouve. **Après** quelques stations, elles arrivent à Bellecour, où beaucoup de gens descendent avec elles. C'est l'une des stations les plus importantes de la ville, parce que les gens y changent de ligne ou y descendent pour aller **travailler** dans la zone.

Acheter (verbe) : to buy
S'asseoir (verbe) : to sit down
Jamais (adverbe) : never
Plus (adverbe) : more
Toujours (adverbe) : always
Tant que (locution adverbiale) : as long as
Après (préposition) : after
Où (adverbe) : where

Travailler (verbe) : to work

Clara est impressionnée par ce qu'elle voit en sortant du métro. L'architecture magnifique des **bâtiments**, et les gens si bien **habillés** ! Elles continuent leur chemin vers Paul, et Clara s'étonne de toutes les choses qu'elle voit dans cette ville. Quand elles arrivent au lieu de rendez-vous, elles sont un peu en avance, alors elles décident d'en profiter pour prendre un petit **quelque chose** à **manger**.

Bâtiment (m) (nom commun) : building
Habillé (adjectif) : dressed
Quelque chose (pronom) : something
Manger (verbe) : to eat

- Bonjour, qu'est-ce que je vous sers ? **demande** le **serveur**.

- Un chocolat **chaud** et un croissant pour moi, dit Clara, pendant que Céline **commande** un cappuccino et un pain au chocolat.

- Très bien, ça fait huit euros **soixante-dix**.

- Cette fois c'est moi qui paye, comme c'est ton **premier jour** ! dit Céline.

- Oh, tu es trop gentille !

Demander (verbe) : to ask
Serveur (m) (nom commun) : waiter
Chaud (adjectif) : hot, warm
Commander (verbe) : to order
Soixante-dix (m) (nom commun) : seventy
Premier (adjectif) : first
Jour (m) (nom commun) : day

Les filles prennent leurs **boissons** et leurs pâtisseries, et vont trouver une table où s'installer. Peu de temps après, les amis de Céline arrivent et les **rejoignent** à la table.

- Bonjour **tout le monde** ! Céline les salue en leur faisant la bise, un rapide **bisou** sur chaque **joue**. Voilà mon amie de New York, Clara, elle va habiter avec moi pendant quelques **mois**. Pour le moment elle est **un peu timide**, mais elle aimerait bien pratiquer son français avec vous. Mettons nous autour de la table et présentons nous les uns après les autres ! suggère Céline.

Boisson (f) (nom commun) : drink
Rejoindre (verbe) : to join
Tout le monde (locution) : everybody
Bisou (m) (nom commun) : kiss
Joue (f) (nom commun) : cheek
Mois (m) (nom commun) : a month
Un peu (adverbe) : a bit
Timide (adjectif) : shy

- Salut, je m'appelle Léonie et j'ai 15 ans. Mes parents sont allemands **mais** vivent ici, et j'ai habité en France toute ma vie. C'est cool parce que chez moi je parle allemand, mais avec mes amis je parle français !

- Bonjour, moi je m'appelle Adam, j'ai 15 ans aussi, je suis français. Ma famille **vient** du Sud de la France, d'une ville qui s'appelle Antibes et qui se trouve juste **à côté de** Nice.

- Bonjour, je m'appelle María. J'ai 16 ans, je suis espagnole. Je suis en France pour un an, moi aussi je suis là pour **améliorer** mon français !

Wow ! Clara est surprise par la **gentillesse** des amis de Céline, et par leurs différences. Après quelques minutes à **bavarder**, elle se sent déjà **à l'aise** et beaucoup plus sûre de son français. Elle n'est plus du tout inquiète.

Mais (conjonction) : but
Venir (verbe) : to come from
À côté de (locution adverbiale) : next to
Améliorer (verbe) : to improve
Gentillesse (f) (nom commun) : kindness
Bavarder (verbe) : to chat
À l'aise (locution adverbiale) : to be comfortable

Questions (Chapitre 1)

1) Où se retrouvent les amis de Céline ?

    a) Chez MacDo

    b) Chez Paul

    c) Chez Starbucks

    d) Chez Pomme de Pain

2) En quelle saison sommes-nous ?

    a) L'été

    b) Le printemps

    c) L'automne

    d) L'hiver

3) À quelle station descendent-elles ?

    a) Bellecour

    b) Hôtel de Ville

    c) Garibaldi

    d) Grange Blanche

4) Qu'est-ce que Clara commande ?

    a) Un latte

    b) Un capuccino

    c) Un chocolat chaud

    d) Un café au lait

5) D'où vient Adam ?

    a) De Nice

    b) D'Allemagne

    c) D'Espagne

    d) D'Antibes

Nouvelle vie, nouvelle aventure

Clara est une jeune américaine originaire de New York qui vient d'arriver en France, plus précisément à Lyon, où elle va passer un an. Elle s'installe chez Céline Crespo, sa correspondante depuis plus d'un an. Clara est un peu inquiète, parce que c'est la première fois qu'elle est si loin de chez elle et aussi parce qu'elle se sent un peu préoccupée par son niveau de français. Céline propose de lui présenter ses amis, qui sont très sympas et accueillants, et avec qui elle va pouvoir pratiquer son français.

Par chance, c'est le week-end, les amis de Céline sont donc disponibles pour se réunir. Ils décident de se retrouver chez Paul, une chaîne de boulangeries qui fait de très bonnes pâtisseries. Le rendez-vous est à 14h, et il est seulement midi, elles ont donc un peu de temps à perdre. Clara pense qu'il serait bien de faire un petit tour en ville et de prendre le métro, pour découvrir son fonctionnement. On n'est pas encore en hiver, mais il fait vraiment froid ce jour-là : elles enfilent des vêtements chauds, mettent leurs manteaux et sortent.

"Ma maison est environ à 20

New life, new adventure

Clara is a young American from New York who has just arrived in France, in Lyon to be precise, where she will spend a year. She moves in with Céline Crespo, who has been her pen pal for over a year. Clara is a little worried, because it was is her first time so far from home, and also a little concerned about her level of French. Céline offers to introduce her to her friends, who are very nice and welcoming, and with whom she will be able to practice her French.

Luckily it's the weekend, so Céline's friends are available to get together. They decide to meet at Paul's, a chain of bakeries that make very good pastries. The meeting is at 2 p.m., and it's only midday, so they have a little time to spare. Clara thinks that it would be good to take a little walk in the city and to take the subway to see how it works. It's not winter yet, but today it's really cold: they put on warm clothes, put on their coats, and go out.

"My house is about 20 minutes

85

minutes de la station Hôtel de Ville, où on va retrouver les copains," explique Céline à Clara. "On est à Garibaldi, et on doit changer de métro à Bellecour, qui est au centre-ville."

"Puisqu'on a le temps, pourquoi ne pas marcher à partir de Bellecour, comme ça je découvre un peu la ville," propose Clara.

Céline trouve l'idée très bonne, et elles se mettent en route.

"Le métro fonctionne très bien à Lyon : il est facile à utiliser, et c'est quasiment impossible de se perdre ! Par exemple, pour acheter un ticket, tu dois simplement trouver une machine, il y en a dans toutes les stations, sélectionner le ticket dont tu as besoin ce jour-là, et payer par carte ou en liquide. Voilà, le ticket s'imprime immédiatement et sera vérifié automatiquement en passant les portillons du métro," explique Céline.

Elles achètent toutes les deux leurs tickets et s'assoient en attendant l'arrivée du métro. Céline explique à Clara qu'il y a beaucoup de métro qui passent à toute heure, et qu'on n'attend donc jamais plus de quelques minutes. C'est l'un des points positifs de ce moyen de transport !

from Hôtel de Ville station, where we are going to meet my friends," Céline explains to Clara. "We're at Garibaldi, and we have to change metro at Bellecour, which is downtown."

"Since we have time, why don't we walk from Bellecour, so I can discover the city a little," suggests Clara.

Céline thinks that it is a very good idea, and they set off.

"The metro works very well in Lyon: it's easy to use, and it's almost impossible to get lost! For example, to buy a ticket you just have to find a machine, there are some in every station, select the ticket you need that day, and pay by card or cash. That's it, the ticket is printed immediately and will be checked automatically when passing through the metro gates," explains Céline.

They both buy their tickets, and sit down waiting for the subway to arrive. Céline explains to her that at any time of the day, there are lots of subways, so we never wait more than a few minutes. It is one of the positive points of this means of transport!

Dans chaque wagon, il y a un panneau qui représente la ligne de métro, comme ça on sait toujours quel est le prochain arrêt. Tant qu'on y fait attention, on sait toujours où on se trouve. Après quelques stations, elles arrivent à Bellecour, où beaucoup de gens descendent avec elles. C'est l'une des stations les plus importantes de la ville, parce que les gens y changent de ligne ou y descendent pour aller travailler dans la zone.	In each carriage, there is a poster which represents the line of the subway so that we always know which is the next stop. As long as you pay attention to that, you always know where you are. After a few stations, they arrive at Bellecour, where many people get off with them. It's one of the most important stations in the city because people change lines or get off there to go to work in the area.
Clara est impressionnée par ce qu'elle voit en sortant du métro. L'architecture magnifique des bâtiments, et les gens si bien habillés ! Elles continuent leur chemin vers Paul, et Clara s'étonne de toutes les choses qu'elle voit dans cette ville. Quand elles arrivent au lieu de rendez-vous, elles sont un peu en avance, alors elles décident d'en profiter pour prendre un petit quelque chose à manger.	Clara is impressed by what she sees when she gets out of the subway. The beautiful architecture of the buildings, and the people so well dressed! They continue on their way to Paul, and Clara is amazed at all the things she sees in this city. When they arrive at the meeting place, they are a little early, so they decide to take advantage and have a little something to eat.
"Bonjour, qu'est-ce que je vous sers ?" demande le serveur.	"Hello, what can I get you?" asks the waiter.
"Un chocolat chaud et un croissant pour moi," dit Clara, pendant que Céline commande un cappuccino et un pain au chocolat.	"A hot chocolate and a croissant for me," says Clara, while Céline orders a cappuccino and a pain au chocolat.
"Très bien, ça fait huit euros soixante-dix."	"Very well, that's eight euros seventy."
"Cette fois c'est moi qui paye,	"This time it's me who pays, as it's

comme c'est ton premier jour ! dit Céline.

"Oh, tu es trop gentille !"

Les filles prennent leurs boissons et leurs pâtisseries, et vont trouver une table où s'installer. Peu de temps après, les amis de Céline arrivent et les rejoignent à la table.

"Bonjour tout le monde !" Céline les salue en leur faisant la bise, un rapide bisou sur chaque joue. "Voilà mon amie de New York, Clara, elle va habiter avec moi pendant quelques mois. Pour le moment elle est un peu timide, mais elle aimerait bien pratiquer son français avec vous. Mettons nous autour de la table et présentons nous les uns après les autres !" suggère Céline.

"Salut, je m'appelle Léonie et j'ai 15 ans. Mes parents sont allemands mais vivent ici, et j'ai habité en France toute ma vie. C'est cool parce que chez moi je parle allemand, mais avec mes amis je parle français !"

"Bonjour, moi je m'appelle Adam, j'ai 15 ans aussi, je suis français. Ma famille vient du Sud de la France, d'une ville qui s'appelle Antibes et qui se trouve juste à côté de Nice."

"Bonjour, je m'appelle María. J'ai 16 ans, je suis espagnole. Je suis en

your first day!" says Céline.

"Oh, you are too nice!"

The girls take their drinks and pastries, and go find a table to sit at. Soon after, Céline's friends arrive and join them at the table.

"Hello everybody!" Céline greets them with a quick kiss on each cheek. "This is my friend from New York, Clara, she is going to live with me for a few months. At the moment she is a bit shy, but she would like to practice her French with you. Let's get around the table and introduce ourselves one after the other!" suggests Céline.

"Hi, my name is Léonie and I'm 15 years old. My parents are German but live here, so I've lived in France all my life. It's cool because at home I speak German, but with my friends I speak French!"

"Hello, my name is Adam, I'm 15 years old too, I'm French. My family comes from the South of France, from a town called Antibes, which is just next to Nice."

"Hello, my name is María. I'm 16 years old, I'm Spanish. I'm in France

France pour un an, moi aussi je suis là pour améliorer mon français ! "

Wow ! Clara est surprise par la gentillesse des amis de Céline, et par leurs différences. Après quelques minutes à bavarder, elle se sent déjà à l'aise et beaucoup plus sûre de son français. Elle n'est plus du tout inquiète.

for a year, I'm here to improve my French too!"

Wow! Clara is surprised by the kindness of Céline's friends, and by their differences. After a few minutes of chatting, she already feels at ease and much more confident about her French. She's not worried at all.

Questions (Chapitre 1)

1) Où se retrouvent les amis de Céline ?

    a) Chez MacDo

    b) Chez Paul

    c) Chez Starbucks

    d) Chez Pomme de Pain

2) En quelle saison sommes-nous ?

    a) L'été

    b) Le printemps

    c) L'automne

    d) L'hiver

3) À quelle station descendent-elles ?

    a) Bellecour

    b) Hôtel de Ville

    c) Garibaldi

    d) Grange Blanche

4) Qu'est-ce que Clara commande ?

    a) Un latte

    b) Un capuccino

    c) Un chocolat chaud

    d) Un café au lait

5) D'où vient Adam ?

    a) De Nice

    b) D'Allemagne

Questions (Chapter 1)

1) Where do Céline's friends meet?

    a) At MacDo's

    b) Paul's

    c) Starbucks

    d) At Pomme de Pain

2) What season is it?

    a) Summer

    b) Spring

    c) Fall

    d) Winter

3) Which station do they go down to?

    a) Bellecour

    b) Hôtel de Ville

    c) Garibaldi

    d) Grange Blanche

4) What does Clara order?

    a) A latte

    b) A cappuccino

    c) A hot chocolate

    d) A coffee with milk

5) Where is Adam from?

    a) From Nice

    b) Germany

c) D'Espagne
d) D'Antibes

c) Spain
d) From Antibes

Chapitre 2 - Le début de l'année scolaire

Demain est un grand jour : c'est **la rentrée des classes**. Dans les premiers jours de septembre, tous les enfants français **retournent** à l'école. Clara est très impatiente de **découvrir** le lycée ! Céline lui a expliqué que l'école française se fait en quatre **étapes** : la maternelle pour les petits entre trois et cinq ans, puis la primaire pour les enfants qui ont entre six et dix ans, ensuite le collège pour les enfants de onze à quatorze ans, et enfin le lycée pour les adolescents de quinze à dix-huit ans. Céline et Clara vont entrer au lycée ensemble. Le petit frère de Céline, Matéo, est encore au collège. Il a seulement treize ans.

Pour se préparer, toute la famille va au **supermarché** pour acheter les **fournitures scolaires**. Il y a beaucoup de monde ! La mère de Céline, Florence, a fait une liste des choses à acheter.

- Bon, on va commencer par choisir un nouveau **sac-à-dos** pour Matéo, parce que celui de l'année **dernière** est cassé. Qu'est-ce que tu penses de ce sac-à-dos Spiderman ? demande Florence.

- Mais c'est pour les bébés ! Je veux un sac normal, comme **celui-là**. Il est complètement noir, et il est cool, répond Matéo.

- Bon, comme tu veux ! Maintenant, choisissez tous un agenda. Faites attention, il doit être assez grand pour pouvoir écrire tous vos **devoirs**, ajoute Florence.

- Je n'ai pas envie d'avoir des devoirs tous les soirs… Pourquoi est-ce que les vacances ne durent pas toujours ? se plaint Céline.

Rentrée des classes (f) (locution nominale) : the start of the school year
Retourner à (verbe) : to come back to
Découvrir (verbe) : to discover
Étape (f) (nom commun) : step
Supermarché (m) (nom commun) : supermarket
Fournitures scolaires (f, pl) (nom commun) : school supplies
Sac-à-dos (m) (nom commun) : backpack
Dernier (adjectif) : last
Celui-là (pronom) : that one
Agenda (m) (nom commun) : diary
Devoirs (m, pl) (nom commun) : homework

Après les agendas, ils vont chercher des **cahiers**, des **stylos** et des **crayons**. Un **stylo-plume**, un stylo rouge, un stylo vert, un **surligneur**, et des crayons à papier pour faire les exercices. Ils achètent aussi des **crayons de couleur** et de la **peinture** pour le cours d'arts plastiques. Pour le cours de sport, ils ont besoin d'un **survêtement** et de **baskets**. Tous les ans, en septembre, les supermarchés proposent toutes ces choses : pas besoin d'aller dans différents magasins. C'est plus pratique ! Il y a même des **blouses blanches** pour le cours de **chimie** des filles. Tout ce **matériel scolaire**, cela représente beaucoup d'**argent**.

Cahier (m) (nom commun) : notebook
Stylo (m) (nom commun) : pen
Crayon (à papier) (m) (nom commun) : pencil
Stylo-plume (m) (nom commun) : fountain pen
Surligneur (m) (nom commun) : highlighter

Crayon de couleur (m) (nom commun) : colored pencil
Peinture (f) (nom commun) : paint
Survêtement (m) (nom commun) : tracksuit
Baskets (f, pl) (nom commun) : sneakers
Blouse blanche (f) (nom commun) : lab coat
Chimie (f) (nom commun) : chemistry
Matériel scolaire (m) (nom commun) : school supplies
Argent (m) (nom commun) : money

Le soir, les enfants vont tous **se coucher tôt**. Et le lendemain, quand le **réveil sonne** à six heures quarante cinq, Clara **se réveille** difficilement ! Elle **s'habille, se coiffe,** et va prendre son **petit déjeuner**. Céline est déjà installée à table, avec un bol de chocolat chaud et des **tartines**. Clara se prépare un café au lait, et fait griller du pain pour se faire des tartines. Les français mangent leurs tartines avec du **beurre**, de la **confiture**, ou du Nutella. Mais Clara a apporté un pot de **beurre de cacahuètes** pour se sentir comme à la maison ! Grâce à elle, Matéo en a goûté pour la première fois, et maintenant il en mange tous les matins.

Se coucher (verbe) : to go to bed
Tôt (adverbe) : early
Réveil (m) (nom commun) : alarm clock
Sonner (verbe) : to ring
Se réveiller (verbe) : to wake up
S'habiller (verbe) : to dress
Se coiffer (verbe) : to make one's hair
Petit déjeuner (m) (nom commun) : breakfast
Tartine (f) (nom commun) : toast
Beurre (m) (nom commun) : butter
Confiture (f) (nom commun) : jam
Beurre de cacahuète (m) (nom commun) : peanut butter
Goûter (verbe) : to taste, to try some food

Sur le chemin de l'école, les filles **retrouvent** María, qui habite à côté. Quand elles arrivent au lycée, Clara est un peu impressionnée par tous ces gens qu'elle ne connaît pas. Heureusement, dans la **cour de**

récréation, elle reconnaît rapidement les amis de Céline. Sur un **mur**, la liste des cours et la **répartition** par salles de classes sont affichés. Elle trouve aussi les horaires d'ouverture des **secrétariats** et de la bibliothèque universitaire. En théorie, les cours commencent à 8 heures - mais cela dépend de l'agenda et du cursus que l'on a choisi.

Retrouver (verbe) : to meet
Cour de récréation (f) (nom commun) : schoolyard
Mur (m) (nom commun) : wall
Répartition (f) (nom commun) : distribution
Secrétariat (m) (nom commun) : secretarial office

Tous les élèves de la classe se présentent. La nationalité de Clara **attire** beaucoup **l'attention** ! Ils lui posent beaucoup de questions, ils veulent tout savoir sur sa vie aux États-Unis. Le professeur distribue les **emplois du temps**, et Clara est contente de voir que, le mardi, ils ne commencent qu'à dix heures : elle va pouvoir **se lever** un peu plus tard !

Le midi, tout le monde mange à la **cantine** : en France, l'école organise et sert le **repas** des élèves. Les menus sont validés par le **conseil d'administration** et par un nutritionniste. En entrée, Clara choisit une salade d'**endives**, parce qu'elle n'en jamais goûté auparavant. Comme plat principal, elle prend du **poisson** avec de la **purée** et des **haricots verts**. Et, en dessert, on peut choisir un **produit laitier** et un fruit ou un **gâteau**.

- Pourquoi il y a des assiettes de fromage en dessert ? demande Clara.

- En France, traditionnellement, on mange le fromage **entre** le plat et le dessert. Aujourd'hui, il y a du camembert et du gruyère, c'est très bon. Moi, je prends ça, et une **part** de gâteau aux **amandes**, dit Céline.

Attirer l'attention (locution verbale) : to draw attention
Emploi du temps (m) (nom commun) : schedule
Se lever (verbe) : to get up
Cantine (f) (nom commun) : canteen
Repas (m) (nom commun) : meal
Conseil d'administration (m) (nom commun) : school board
Endive (f) (nom commun) : chicory

Poisson (m) (nom commun) : fish
Purée (f) (nom commun) : mashed potatoes
Haricot vert (m) (nom commun) : green bean
Produit laitier (m) (nom commun) : dairy product
Gâteau (m) (nom commun) : cake
Entre (préposition) : between
Part (f) (nom commun) : slice
Amande (f) (nom commun) : almond

Questions (Chapitre 2)

1) Comment s'appelle l'école pour un adolescent de 17 ans ?

    a) La maternelle

    b) L'école primaire

    c) Le collège

    d) Le lycée

2) Comment s'appelle l'école pour un enfant de 13 ans ?

    a) La maternelle

    b) L'école primaire

    c) Le collège

    d) Le lycée

3) Que mange Clara pour le petit déjeuner ?

    a) Un chocolat chaud et des tartines de beurre

    b) Un café au lait et des tartines de confiture

    c) Un café au lait et des tartines de beurre de cacahuètes

    d) Un chocolat chaud et des tartines de beurre de cacahuètes

4) À quelle heure commencent vraiment les cours ?

    a) Six heures quarante-cinq

    b) Huit heures trente

    c) Huit heures dix

    d) Huit heures

5) Comment s'organise le repas du midi dans les écoles françaises ?

    a) Les enfants apportent leurs sandwiches

    b) Les enfants vont dans un restaurant à côté de l'école

    c) Les enfants rentrent chez eux

    d) Les enfants vont à la cantine de l'école

Le début de l'année scolaire

Demain est un grand jour : c'est la rentrée des classes. Dans les premiers jours de septembre, tous les enfants français retournent à l'école. Clara est très impatiente de découvrir le lycée ! Céline lui a expliqué que l'école française se fait en quatre étapes : la maternelle pour les petits entre trois et cinq ans, puis la primaire pour les enfants qui ont entre six et dix ans, ensuite le collège pour les enfants de onze à quatorze ans, et enfin le lycée pour les adolescents de quinze à dix-huit ans. Céline et Clara vont entrer au lycée ensemble. Le petit frère de Céline, Matéo, est encore au collège. Il a seulement treize ans.

Pour se préparer, toute la famille va au supermarché pour acheter les fournitures scolaires. Il y a beaucoup de monde ! La mère de Céline, Florence, a fait une liste des choses à acheter.

"Bon, on va commencer par choisir un nouveau sac-à-dos pour Matéo, parce que celui de l'année dernière est cassé. Qu'est-ce que tu penses de ce sac-à-dos Spiderman ?" demande Florence.

"Mais c'est pour les bébés ! Je veux un sac normal, comme celui-là.

The beginning of the school year

Tomorrow is a big day: it's the start of the school year. In the first days of September, all French children come back to school. Clara is very impatient to discover the high school! Céline explained to her that the French school has four stages: kindergarten, for children between three and five years old, then primary school for kids between six and ten, next is middle school for children aged eleven to fourteen, and high school for adolescents aged fifteen to eighteen. Céline and Clara will enter high school together. Céline's little brother Matéo is still in college. He's only thirteen.

To prepare, the whole family goes to the supermarket to buy school supplies. There are a lot of people! Céline's mother, Florence, has a list of all the things to buy.

"Well, we'll start by choosing a new backpack for Matéo, because last year's one is broken. What do you think of this Spiderman backpack?" asks Florence.

"But it's for babies! I want a normal bag, like that one. It's completely

Il est complètement noir, et il est cool," répond Matéo.

"Bon, comme tu veux ! Maintenant, choisissez tous un agenda. Faites attention, il doit être assez grand pour pouvoir écrire tous vos devoirs," ajoute Florence.

"Je n'ai pas envie d'avoir des devoirs tous les soirs… Pourquoi est-ce que les vacances ne durent pas toujours ?" se plaint Céline.

Après les agendas, ils vont chercher des cahiers, des stylos et des crayons. Un stylo-plume, un stylo rouge, un stylo vert, un surligneur, et des crayons à papier pour faire les exercices. Ils achètent aussi des crayons de couleur et de la peinture pour le cours d'arts plastiques. Pour le cours de sport, ils ont besoin d'un survêtement et de baskets. Tous les ans, en septembre, les supermarchés proposent toutes ces choses : pas besoin d'aller dans différents magasins. C'est plus pratique ! Il y a même des blouses blanches pour le cours de chimie des filles. Tout ce matériel scolaire, cela représente beaucoup d'argent.

Le soir, les enfants vont tous se coucher tôt. Et le lendemain, quand le réveil sonne à six heures quarante cinq, Clara se réveille difficilement ! Elle s'habille, se coiffe, et va prendre son petit

black, and it's cool," replies Matéo.

"As you wish! Now you all have to do is choose a diary. Be careful, it must be large enough to be able to write all your homework," adds Florence.

"I don't feel like having homework every night… Why don't the holidays last forever?" complains Céline.

After the diaries, they go to get notebooks, pens and pencils. A fountain pen, a red pen, a green pen, a highlighter, and pencils for doing the exercises. They also buy colored pencils and paint for the art class. For the sports class, they need a tracksuit, and sneakers. Every year in September, supermarkets carry all of these things: you don't have to go to different stores. It is more convenient! There are even white lab coats for the girls' chemistry class. All this school supplies means a lot of money.

Tonight the kids all go to bed early. When the alarm clock rings at six forty five, Clara wakes up with difficulty! She' gets dressed, makes her hair, and goes to have breakfast. Céline is already seated

déjeuner. Céline est déjà installée à table, avec un bol de chocolat chaud et des tartines. Clara se prépare un café au lait, et fait griller du pain pour se faire des tartines. Les français mangent leurs tartines avec du beurre, de la confiture, ou du Nutella. Mais Clara a apporté un pot de beurre de cacahuètes pour se sentir comme à la maison ! Grâce à elle, Matéo en a goûté pour la première fois, et maintenant il en mange tous les matins.

Sur le chemin de l'école, les filles retrouvent María, qui habite à côté. Quand elles arrivent au lycée, Clara est un peu impressionnée par tous ces gens qu'elle ne connaît pas. Heureusement, dans la cour de récréation, elle reconnaît rapidement les amis de Céline. Sur un mur, la liste des cours et la répartition par salles de classes sont affichés. Elle trouve aussi les horaires d'ouverture des secrétariats et de la bibliothèque universitaire. En théorie, les cours commencent à 8 heures - mais cela dépend de l'agenda et du cursus que l'on a choisi.

Tous les élèves de la classe se présentent. La nationalité de Clara attire beaucoup l'attention ! Ils lui posent beaucoup de questions, ils veulent tout savoir sur sa vie aux États-Unis. Le professeur distribue les emplois du temps, et Clara est

at the table, with a bowl of hot chocolate and toast. Clara prepares a coffee with milk and toasts bread for herself. The French eat their sandwiches with butter, jam, or Nutella. But Clara brought a jar of peanut butter to make her feel right at home! Matéo first tasted peanut butter thanks to her, and now he eats it every morning.

On the way, the girls meet María, who lives nearby. When they get to high school, Clara is a bit in awe of all these people she doesn't know. Fortunately, in the schoolyard she quickly recognizes Céline's friends. On a wall, the list of courses and the distribution by classrooms are posted. She also finds the opening hours of the secretarial office and the university library. In theory, classes start at 8 a.m. - but it depends on the schedule and the course of study.

All the students in the class introduce themselves. Clara's nationality draws a lot of attention! They ask her a lot of questions, they want to know everything about her life in the United States. The teacher distributes the schedule, Clara is

contente de voir que, le mardi, ils ne commencent qu'à dix heures : elle va pouvoir se lever un peu plus tard !	happy to see that on Tuesday they start at ten o'clock: she will be able to wake up a little later!
Le midi, tout le monde mange à la cantine : en France, l'école organise et sert le repas des élèves. Les menus sont validés par le conseil d'administration et par un nutritionniste. En entrée, Clara choisit une salade d'endives, parce qu'elle n'en jamais goûté auparavant. Comme plat principal, elle prend du poisson avec de la purée et des haricots verts. Et, en dessert, on peut choisir un produit laitier et un fruit ou un gâteau.	At noon, everyone eats in the canteen: in France, the school organizes and serves meals for the students. The menus are validated by the school board of directors and by a nutritionist. As a starter, Clara chooses an chicory salad because she has never tasted it before. As a main course, she takes fish with mashed potatoes and green beans. And for dessert, you can choose a dairy product and a fruit or cake.
"Pourquoi il y a des assiettes de fromage en dessert ?" demande Clara.	"Why are there cheese plates for dessert? asks Clara.
"En France, traditionnellement, on mange le fromage entre le plat et le dessert. Aujourd'hui, il y a du camembert et du gruyère, c'est très bon. Moi, je prends ça, et une part de gâteau aux amandes," dit Céline.	"In France, traditionally, we eat cheese between the main course and the dessert. Today, there is Camembert, and Gruyère, it's very good. I'm going to take this, and a slice of almond cake," says Céline.

Questions (Chapitre 2)

1) Comment s'appelle l'école pour un adolescent de 17 ans ?

   a) La maternelle

   b) L'école primaire

   c) Le collège

   d) Le lycée

2) Comment s'appelle l'école pour un enfant de 13 ans ?

   a) La maternelle

   b) L'école primaire

   c) Le collège

   d) Le lycée

3) Que mange Clara pour le petit déjeuner ?

   a) Un chocolat chaud et des tartines de beurre

   b) Un café au lait et des tartines de confiture

   c) Un café au lait et des tartines de beurre de cacahuètes

   d) Un chocolat chaud et des tartines de beurre de cacahuètes

4) À quelle heure commencent vraiment les cours ?

   a) Six heures quarante-cinq

   b) Huit heures trente

   c) Huit heures dix

   d) Huit heures

Questions (Chapter 2)

1) What is school called for a 17 year old?

   a) Kindergarden

   b) Primary school

   c) College

   d) High school

2) What is school called for a 13 year old?

   a) Kindergarden

   b) Primary school

   c) College

   d) High school

3) What does Clara eat for breakfast?

   a) Hot chocolate and butter toast

   b) A coffee with milk and jam toast

   c) A coffee with milk and peanut butter toast

   d) Hot chocolate and peanut butter toast

4) What time do classes really start?

   a) Six forty-five

   b) Eight-thirty

   c) Ten past eight

   d) Eight o'clock

5) **Comment s'organise le repas du midi dans les écoles françaises ?**

   a) Les enfants apportent leurs sandwiches

   b) Les enfants vont dans un restaurant à côté de l'école

   c) Les enfants rentrent chez eux

   d) Les enfants vont à la cantine de l'école

5) **How is the midday meal organized in French schools?**

   a) Children bring their sandwich

   b) The children go to a restaurant next to the school

   c) The children go home

   d) The children go to the school canteen

Les Réponses

Chapitre 1

1) b
2) c
3) a
4) c
5) d

Chapitre 2

1) d
2) c
3) c
4) d
5) d

Answers

Chapter 1

1) b
2) c
3) a
4) c
5) d

Chapter 2

1) d
2) c
3) c
4) d
5) d

Want to receive a fun weekly email on all things French? It will include topics such as culture, festivals, facts, stories, and idioms. Scan the QR code below to join!

www.ingramcontent.com/pod-product-compliance
Lightning Source LLC
Chambersburg PA
CBHW071744080526
44588CB00013B/2143